Writing and Reading
George Bowering

Writing and Reading
George Bowering

ESSAYS

VANCOUVER | NEW STAR BOOKS | 2019

Copyright George Bowering 2019. All rights reserved. No part of this work may be reproduced, stored in a retrieval system or transmitted, in any form or by any means, without the prior written consent of the publisher or a licence from the Canadian Copyright Licensing Agency (Access Copyright).

✺

New Star Books Ltd.
www.NewStarBooks.com | info@NewStarBooks.com

No. 107 – 3477 Commercial St., Vancouver, BC V5N 4E8 CANADA
1574 Gulf Road, No. 1517, Point Roberts, WA 98281 USA

The publisher acknowledges the financial support of the Canada Council for the Arts and the British Columbia Arts Council.

Canada Council for the Arts | Conseil des arts du Canada   BRITISH COLUMBIA ARTS COUNCIL   BRITISH COLUMBIA

Cataloguing information for this book is available from Library and Archives Canada, collectionscanada.gc.ca

Cover & interior design by Robin Mitchell Cranfield

Printed & bound in Canada by Imprimerie Gauvin, Gatineau, QC
First printing, November 2019

Contents

That Blank Page 1

Oliver 2

Those Sentence Poems. 3

Poly Oana craquer 4

Tough Times and the Arts 6

Pages I Have Trouble With 3: Grappa 7

Collections 9

Showing The Battle of Algiers *to Younger Hipper Moviegoers* 11

Seems Like Happiness 13

Kroetsch Listens 15

The Holy Life of the Intellect 17

Letters from Mike 19

Alice Munro 21

Cloud Atlas 23

Fitz 25

Look at That 28

Hooray, Difficulty! 31

Notes on "I Like Summer" 34

How I Wrote Mirror on the Floor 37

The Playwright Whose Name Rimes with the Title of His Most Famous Play 40

Well, Rosenblatt 43

Six Answers for Rebecca Tuck, Who Asked about Greg Curnoe and Me 47

Letter to Peter DeLottinville 51

In In the Skin 56

He's Up Again! 61

My Heart in Hiding 66

He Gets Better Every Year 73

The Objects of My Affection 81

1967 Books 90

Apollinaire and Vancouver: A Story about Our Poetry 112

Those Young Rimbauds: A Discussion about Writing and Reading 137

Acknowledgments 163

Index 164

That Blank Page

When you sit down to write a novel, and you are facing that proverbial blank page, you may as well have been plunked down in a country whose language you don't know. The language you are going to try to work with is useless. All you can hope is that you will come up with something that seems powerful, and something more rare than that — beautiful. In that case, you will not be comfortable, but you will be on your way to citizenry. When you sit down to read a novel, well, where are you?

Oliver

When we went down to the Oliver Theatre on a Saturday afternoon to see a western movie in colour, we saw the same landscape we would see the next day, when we went for a hike in the hills on either side of the valley. We were careful about where we put a foot down, because of cactus, because of rattlesnake, because of animal poop that hadn't been baked yet. A semi-arid climate, we were told in school; yet there were wet slugs in the long grass around the trunks of cherry trees. There were pheasants with eggs or chicks in that long grass too, and our young hearts would just about stop for the sudden noise when those big birds took to the treetops. The shade of those trees made wonderful respite when the sun's blaze went to three figures on the Fahrenheit scale. We boys took our shirts off when school let us out in late June, and didn't put them back on till they made us go back in for September. Nobody's house or car had air conditioning, and neither did the stores and pool halls on the main drag, also known as Highway 97. It rained hard one July day every year, just in time to ruin the cherry crop, and again on a Sunday in September, so a guy could sleep in instead of picking apples all day. Now I have been living in cities for sixty-five years, some of them on other continents, but I drive up to the south Okanagan every August, and when I get my first glimpse of dry hills and rock slides I say "This is how it's supposed to be."

Those Sentence Poems.

Naturally, as time goes by and you are still a poet, you get asked to contribute toward some kind of celebration of another poet. Perhaps the poet has reached a certain age — fifty, or seventy, let us say. Sometimes the poet has just died, and words are required. Maybe the poet is getting married, or asked into the Order of Canada, or delivered of a job the poet has always hated. Many years ago, when it began to look as if written tributes would keep on being required, I decided to stick with a form I may have invented. The poem would consist of a number of sentences, always a little over a line in length but not as long as three lines. The sentences would not develop any theme or argument, but just follow on one another until they had all happened. I have written a lot of these poems, and they have been published in newspapers, anthologies, one-off birthday presents, and as time went by, my collections of poems. I have written them for Louis Dudek, Allen Ginsberg and Leonard Cohen. "A Step this Side of Salvation" was written for a seventieth birthday party some good folk threw for David McFadden in Toronto. "Eh You" was written for a life celebration, complete with the best chopped chicken livers I have ever tasted at The Word bookstore in Montreal a few months after Artie Gold died. "Nechako Spring Morning" was written for Sharon Thesen, but I don't remember what the occasion was. It was probably her birthday, but don't expect me to tell you which one.

Poly Oana craquer

Each morning the first thing I do is to read some poetry before getting a coffee and the daily paper's prose. A lot of the books I have tried lately do not disresemble the latter enough. But the work (and play) of Oana Avasilichioaei has raised my hope for the future of our art. We do not really need poems that tell us what the poet saw and how he can make figurative language to give us his view of those things. We do not really need language that is passed over the counter by its baker. Ms Avasilichioaei is environed by language as she is by any world she enters, and when you read you don't read her *version* — you are too busy negotiating the pleasant difficulty of her pages. If you run into one another from time to time? Well, what a nice thing to experience first thing in the morning. This poet offers no Frostian conclusions, but possibilities leading in all directions. Judith Fitzgerald was right when she wrote that you can't really read the poems, but you can sure experience them — and if you do not want poetry to lull you, you will want that experience.

 Oana Avasilichioaei's name is usually preceded or followed by the words poet, translator, editor, collaborator — and you always feel as if all those people are with you while you are experiencing her text. That text can make your eyes jump, maybe into the future. That translator makes you realize that your role is not to consume an English-language text that has replaced a French or Romanian original, but to engage happily with the difficulties of both languages. The poet is not here to enclose but to compose, i.e. to put something beside something. I think that she will continue the work of poets such as Fred Wah and Erín Moure, to waken our ears and imaginations that have been stuffed up with the ordinary.

Tough Times and the Arts

In my lifetime I seem to have gone through lots of times when times were tough, and every time they are, politicians decide that they have to make spending cuts, and every time they do, they make cuts of spending on the arts. They suggest that during serious times you have to take care of serious business, and the arts are really frills. They say we need repaired highways because money comes into the province (or country, or city) on highways. Well, it comes in on stages and in music halls too.
In a recent tough time, taxpayers in Canada, British Columbia and Vancouver involuntarily paid enormous sums to make sure that rich people could watch athletes go downhill on imported snow. Ordinary taxpayers were kept in place by wire fences and large male guards. But over and over honest statisticians have demonstrated that more people assemble and pay more money on the arts than they do on sports. I think that the same people who decide that TV should devote an hour to news, weather and sports, without adding an arts commentator, decide where tax money should go in tough times.

Or look, as people such as I keep on saying, at the big picture. Look at the long run. In 1594 a play called *Romeo and Juliet* was first performed. Does anyone remember any soccer scores from that winter?

Pages I Have Trouble With 3: Grappa

After the airplane takes off, the first thing I do is to turn off the screen in front of me. Then I get out my book and join the minority. But if I am on Air Canada, and if it is my first flight of the month, I like to see whether there is anything to read in *En Route* magazine. It is a pretty classy mag as far as airline mags go, and sometimes there are even articles written by someone I know.

You can't help noticing that there is a kind of contiguity going on in those pages. I mean that if there is an article about Beijing, for example, you will probably find some advertisements for hotels or stores in Beijing. It's something you get used to.

On the way to Edmonton, for example, I had a look through the September 2013 issue. On pages 63 and 64 there was an article entitled "No Sour Grappa," and a translation titled "*Lâche pas la grappa.*" Now, I like grappa. My friend Robert Kroetsch liked grappa. My wife likes grappa, especially in the early afternoon.

So I read the article. It was by someone with a well-known Canadian literary name. Even though the article was shorter than what I would have liked, I enjoyed it. So I tried reading the French translation as well. That's where I ran into a glitch that might have been picked up in proofreading.

In the translation we are told by the author that one night in Venice a novelist friend appeared and invited "ma femme et moi" to his apartment to drink grappa. But in the original English it clearly says that the novelist "invited my wife and I to his apartment."

Clearly, the translator, whose name is not indicated, should have been paying attention. His version should have said that the novelist invited "ma femme et je" to his place. The translator's job is to pay close attention to the original author's understanding of the workings of his native language.

Tut, tut, Air Canada.

Collections

In the collectable Fall 2011 issue of *The Capilano Review*, Donato Mancini has interesting things to say about re-reading. "But 'A poetry collection is like a record collection' (R. Maurer). Bafflement, puzzlement, difference, strangeness, unfamiliarity raise curiosity, invite long-term engagement. 'Love don't come easy' (P. Collins). Poetry is not a consumable. 'It's a game of give and take' (*ibid.*)."

I think that Maurer and Mancini have it nicely right here (except that to my knowledge those quoted song lyrics have to be attributed to The Supremes, if we are talking performers, or Eddie Holland if we are talking writer.)

And/but I think that we could spend a little time on the word "collection." Recently we heard Michael Audain talking about the exhibiting of "The Audain Collection" at the Vancouver Art Gallery. He said that he did not think of his art purchases as a "collection," but rather as repeated instances of the great joy in buying a painting one admires. But remember what Ezra Pound said about art galleries and anthologies? That when you view a room full of paintings you learn about each of them by its proximity to others. This will work whether you have a room full of Picassos, or of *quattrocento* Biblical scenes. You can see where he was going *re* anthologies.

So what about my record collection? Well, one has made an effort to acquire all the great quartets of Beethoven and Coltrane, of course. But there is stuff on those shelves that I have not "added to my collection." I don't know how that Neil Diamond album got in there.

You can see Maurer's point. The poems in a collection, especially if it is not just a hurried hodgepodge, cannot help being related to one another, and like music are likely to grow by being listened to more than once. Maurer means that you don't just rip through a book of poems as if it were an airport novel. You don't even have to (re)read the poems in order: you can listen to Beethoven's late quartets and then go back and put on an early one.

Who made up that phrase, the "canon of representation"? Years ago I thought that "representation" refers not to the art but to the artist. Now Mr. Mancini may have got me thinking that it refers to the reader of the painting or book.

Showing *The Battle of Algiers* to Younger Hipper Moviegoers

For over forty years I have been telling people that Gillo Pontecorvo's *Battle of Algiers* is my favourite movie. But in all those years I have never watched it for a second time. Not until tonight. I am not even sure that I want to see it tonight. Do you get what I mean?

I was a little kid during World War II, and I was in high school during the Korean "police action." I saw many many movies about war. Most of them had Frank Lovejoy and William Bendix in them.

But in the middle of the 1960s I was reading Frantz Fanon and Eldridge Cleaver like everyone else in the university and arts scenes. We had also got used to New Wave film from France, and Fellini and Antonioni from Italy. We were being trained to look at films in a different way. Pontecorvo showed us how to look at war in a different way.

In war movies the British endured the German bombs and sent Jack Hawkins up to the top of the sandbags to murmur, "Gerry's a little restless tonight." Meanwhile the USAmericans drafted wisecracking young football players to head to a Pacific island and wipe out machine-gun nests single-handedly because their buddy had died all in one piece in their arms.

The *Battle of Algiers* didn't offer any of the comforts we'd been taught to accept. There is no protagonist, only human figures who reappear if they are still alive. In fact we couldn't help wondering whether these were actors or the real historical people. It turns out that they were not actors before this film. The camera work took place on site shortly after the end of the war and while the FLN was being challenged for power by other groups. The gunfire and explosions that were taking place in Algiers were often mistaken for the "shooting" of the film.

There were lots of anti-colonialist battles going on in the sixties — in Algeria, Indochina, Angola, Detroit. It seemed like an easy thing to pick sides, especially given the recent romantic story of Cuba. But Pontecorvo, a rich guy who had joined the Communist Party and the Italian Partisans during World War II, will show you French paratroopers and Algerian revolutionaries using terror and torture to press for victory. Pontecorvo shocked the crap out of us long before George W. bin Laden did.

Seems Like Happiness

Irving Layton started one of his most famous poems by saying that he was happiest while writing poetry, and for once in a long while I have to agree with Irving Layton. When a poem has you in its grip you have to shut up all your usual yapping and listen as hard as you can. If it continues to work, and nothing interrupts it, you will get to be the first reader of the poem. It will be a happy event.

Poets are not the only people to know happiness, of course. But I think that one principle operates in poetry and elsewhere — happiness is speechless. If you could describe your happiness you would only corrode it. If you're happy and you know it, clap your hands. When a baseball player who has just arrived at second after hitting a double claps his hands, he is not applauding himself. He is responding to his good luck. Happy and lucky have always been synonyms, haven't they?

Clap your hands. You are too happy for words.

I wonder whether happiness is connected with wisdom. When I was younger people often asked me whether I had had a happy childhood. Apparently this was a normal question to ask people who were undergoing therapy or courtship. I thought about it for a long time, and even wrote about it, but I could never make up my mind for certain. I knew that I felt pretty happy as a child, or so I guessed, but as to my childhood, I wasn't sure. I heard those grownups say that they didn't know that they were poor because they lived just like everyone else in their neighbourhood. I figured it was probably like that regarding happiness.

But now that I am an old gink, I am supposed to have acquired wisdom. I don't know about that, but I can tell you that in recent times I have heard a lot of people tell me that I seem happier than I once appeared. Does this mean that happiness is another name for wisdom? Is that what maturity is? There is a certain irony in wisdom. If you attain it you know that you cannot pass it on. If any young people ask you for the benefit of your wisdom, one thing you know is that the best thing you can say is nothing. Did you ever wonder why old gurus speak in koans?

If you're happy and you know it, clap with one hand.

Kroetsch Listens

Years and years ago I had it figured out that Robert Kroetsch was the writer to read, and looked forward to whatever he might write in my lifetime. The first time I met him was at Government House in 1970. He was getting the Governor General's Award in fiction for *The Studhorse Man*. Then for a year or two I would get to hear him at a festival here and there.

Then one day in the early seventies someone phoned and asked whether I would be Kroetsch's minder for a day. The idea was that I would pick him up at the Vancouver airport, keep him company for several hours, and then drive him to the BC ferry terminal at Horseshoe Bay.

Oh boy! Here was the funniest and smartest writer in the land, and he was on record as being an admirer of the great bullshit artists in prairie beer parlours and horse barns. I'd bring him home and feed him and persuade him to accept a beer and let him loose.

I was married at the time to a very talkative woman. She once admitted, "I didn't know what to say, so I just kept on talking." So when I showed up with Kroetsch she started telling him about everything she had noticed in her life. "Shortly after the start of the Peloponnesian Wars," she said, and off she went. Kroetsch smiled and listened, and more than that, he appeared to enjoy listening. He listened all afternoon, smiling that old-fashioned prairie German-Canadian smile.

I was itching and scratching and rueing my luck. I get my first chance to hear Robert Kroetsch the talker, and he turns out to be a listener.

And that is how I remember Bob. I was lucky enough to hang with him in beer parlours and other sites of culture. We even went on a tour together in the late eighties, visiting universities in Australia and Ontario. That was a dream, I can tell you. I learned a lot during those weeks. But it wasn't easy making Kroetsch do his share of the talking. Chuckling yes; talking not so easy.

That's what Bob Kroetsch was: the great listener. People who sat around a table with him will remember his saying "Is that right?" Or "I'll be darned." Or "No kidding?" Dennis Cooley does a terrific imitation of Kroetsch listening and saying one of these things from time to time.

Kroetsch was a great writer and a great teacher. When he sat there with a bit of a smile and listened, he was teaching you what you needed to learn.

The Holy Life of the Intellect

I believe that the human intellect is the closest thing we have to the divine. It is the way we can join one another in spirit.

Sometimes when you are listening to a great jazz musician performing a long solo, you are experiencing his mind, moment by moment, as it shifts and decides, as it adds and reminds. This happens whether the musician is a saxophone player or a bass player or a pianist. You are in there, where that other mind is. His mind is coming through your ears and inside your mind.

The first time I heard Charlie Parker playing "Ornithology," I was delighted. I was about eleven years old. You are so much alone with your mind as a kid, so when you hear someone else's mind improvising, you feel an excitement you will never get from some music that just wants to keep a steady beat.

I got that delight again when I first heard great improvisatory poetry. When I read *The Desert Music* by William Carlos Williams, the book fell out of my hands and made a loud splat on the library's concrete floor. Later I would hear the poet Philip Whalen call this kind of poetry "a graph of the mind moving." Yes, it is.

It can happen with prose, too — sentences you hear in your head and know how they felt inside another's. I believe that if there is a god, this is what he wanted us to do. It is the holy life of the intellect.

If we can experience another's mind in our own, we know that love is possible. We understand why the great poet Shelley wrote a hymn to what he called "Intellectual Beauty," and called it an invisible power that moves among the things and people of this Earth.

It descended on him when he was a youth looking for wisdom from the words of the dead. Intelligence literally means "choosing among." Shelley called it the spirit of delight. It is the gift of wit, which literally means the kind of seeing that makes you smile and clap your hands together. I believe that this provokes what the Greeks called *agape*, the Romans called *caritas*, and what we settled for as love. It's greater than hope and faith, according to St. Paul of Tarsus in an otherwise questionable letter to the Corinthians.

If you want to hear it happen rather than suffer any more of my apostolic prose, listen to the improvisation by John Coltrane in his immortal album called *A Love Supreme*. There we are: a fine intellect, a tenor saxophone and a reach for perfect prayer.

Letters from Mike

Back in the days of typewriters and envelopes, I used to get great heaps of mail, heaps of mail in my mailbox at school, except for the book packages that would not fit in my mailbox, and great heaps of mail waiting for me at home, and great heaps of mail in the post office box that was a step away from George Woodcock's post office box, where he got great heaps of mail.

In recent years, during the age of digital fooling around and white wires hanging from people's ears, I get virtual mountains of e-mail, but though my heart goes pitter-pat when I hear the mailperson's boots, I don't get the Christmases of letters, books, magazines and postcards I still crave. In the old days and in the more recent days, though, I did get real palpable letters from my lifelong friend Mike Matthews. After Mike left Montreal and fetched up in Nanaimo, after I left Montreal and descended on Vancouver in the very early 1970s, the luminous Matthews-Bowering correspondence began.

By the time that the computers and other artificial stupidity had fully arrived, my correspondence with Mike was one of the few processes that kept me cocking an ear from my side of the front door mail slot. About once a week, sometimes more often, I was able to bellow to my helpmeet, "Yay, a letter from Mike!" Sometimes I would let the letter lie unopened for an hour or more while I pretended to be interested in household tasks such as counting the plates or putting the fridge magnets in alphabetical order.

But then I would gently open the knife drawer, deftly select a blade, and calmly slit the envelope with the inky script in an inelegant hand on the front. The address thus penned would almost always be correct, but the name above this address was usually something such as "Gorgeous Bentbutton."

The page or pages inside would often bear a number of dates, the first one perhaps in computer-printer tidiness, the rest inserted by hand (or foot, I sometimes alleged). The first paragraph was more likely than not to be a tirade against the evil perpetrated by the computer or printer or other nearby device that was expending its energy in a campaign to harass the author of the correspondence. "Oh, you are going to like this one!" I would often shout to my helpmeet Jean.

Those letters were as much fun as Mike's more public rants. Mike Matthews was not, as he claimed, the best fisher on Vancouver Island, but he was the best ranter on Vancouver Island. I'd give anything to have his letters back — and him.

Alice Munro

Two of Canada's great fiction writers lived in British Columbia, so they were not often talked about or written about back in Ontario and points eastward, where the real Canadian Literature was created, as we all know. These writers were Sheila Watson and Ethel Wilson, whose work was produced largely in the 1950s.

Naturally, as a student of Canadian Literature, and a loyal son of British Columbia, I kept pestering the editor of the New Canadian Library, David Staines, to pay more attention to these great women. I bugged him to correct the typical easterners' errors printed on the back cover of *The Double Hook*, and I urged him to publish all of Ethel Wilson's books. The New Canadian Library was much in use by professors and students of our literature, and I hated to see BC's two great novelists fall outside Toronto's attention.

I must have done a lot of pestering, and I must have had a lot of help. One lovely day a new edition of Watson's novel was published, and on the back cover there was no longer the notion that the story took place in the Rocky Mountains. Even more exciting, McClelland & Stewart publishers announced that Ethel Wilson's books would all be published in new editions in the NCL! And I would be extended the honour of writing the afterword to *Swamp Angel*.

In a rare stroke of genius, someone back east decided

to have the launch of these shiny new books in Vancouver, in the West End, in a house that Mrs. Wilson had once lived in. The players from Ontario flew out for the occasion. David Staines was there. Avie Bennett, the wonderful man who had saved M&S from oblivion, was there. The federal minister of culture was there. And Alice Munro, another great British Columbia fiction writer, was there!

I was in West End heaven, I will tell you. A good time was, as they say, had by all. Most of us consumed quite a bit of wine or beer or something. Then we decided that we should all pile into my car and drive to Chinatown for wonderful west coast food and maybe wine or something. I was really not in prime condition to drive, but what could happen with a federal minister in my car?

But most important of all was the walk under the lovely spring trees to my car, parked as it was a few blocks away. Because I got to walk those few blocks with Alice Munro. I got to, as I was always quick to tell Mike Matthews, her greatest fan and the most enthusiastic teacher of her books, walk in the West End under a spring's evening sky with my right arm around Alice Munro. I was the happiest man in Canadian literature.

Cloud Atlas

Recently I saw a male American movie star talking with the comedic host of a midnight television show. The movie star reported that he had been in Germany, working in a movie titled *Cloud Atlas*. The host asked him what it was about. The movie star said that he did not know. Fair enough. The host asked him where the movie idea came from, and the movie star did not seem to know that either. They did not pursue the subject beyond that exchange. My guess is that for every person who reads David Mitchell's novel *Cloud Atlas* there are a million people who recognize the movie star.

  The novel is constructed of six novella-length stories, each of which involves people who are desperately travelling, often being pursued by others who do not wish them well. A cloud atlas is a book of photographs depicting the various kinds of clouds; it is used by weather-watchers, especially those who are travelling by sea or air. The term "cloud atlas" shows up a couple of times in Mitchell's book. In one case it is the title of a musical composition written for six instruments. In the novella titled "Letters from Zedelgheim," a young composer describes his "sextet for overlapping soloists." "In the first set," he writes, "each solo is interrupted by its successor: in the second, each interruption is recontinued, in order."

  That is the structure of the novel, of course, and as

each of the instruments has "its own language of key, scale, and colour," so each novella is set in its own place and time — and genre. We see a nineteenth-century sea story, an epistolary fiction, a satirical British comedy, a post-apocalypse dystopia, and so on. In each novella a character is allowed to read something from the previous narration. And each of these characters bears a peculiar birthmark in the shape of a comet. So it goes: abcdeffedcba.

At first one is put in mind of Italo Calvino's *If on a winter's night a traveller*, and one is inclined to congratulate Mitchell for stepping out of the general everyday meadow or backstreet of standard British fiction. Then one is delighted to catch quick glimpses of other writers, great or domestic. One is encouraged to recall the entire structure and history of literary architecture. And here is the accomplishment I admire most: while David Mitchell took the time to invent a tricky, puzzling, intricate and lengthy machine of experimental writing, he also provided some admirable chase scenes that will have you reading well past your lights-out time. I am not the first reader to attest that I wished for, say, another three novellas in the composition.

Fitz

A few years ago I heard two anecdotal poets curse Judith Fitzgerald's name. Next day I got out my Fitz books and read them again, with added pleasure, part of which was the pleasure of vexation. Anecdotal poetry is made for consumption; more and more, Fitz poetry has been made for reading. The wonderful thing about reading is that the more difficult it becomes, the more enjoyable it can be. A Fitz book ain't a barbecue, and her poems are not burgers. You cannot down them — you might have to curl up with them and hope you have them partly illuminated by morning's light. If you throw poems at the wall when you can't get them right away, pass on. If you love the music even before you figure out the grammar, welcome.

In a country and a time where and when a lot of prominent poets seem to think that it is enough to bring moderate skill to making lyric anecdotes and autobiographical descriptions of events, it is, for me, a great solace and pleasure to see the works of Judith Fitzgerald, and to wish that they could continue to be written. From the beginning she let it be known that for her, poetry is a most serious and necessary art. Her reading was prodigious, and the world of her investigation was always of the highest and most taxing order. Not a musical presentation of a glimpsed seasonal change, but rather a thinking engagement with the great intellectual events that have structured our civilization. In earlier works she took on the thinkers of the ancient world and the medieval one. Later she took on the great modernists, and, characteristically, did so while looking through the frame of an ancient Greek playwright that they themselves availed themselves of.

I have always been interested in Fitzgerald's dedication to the long poem. She knew that a poem would take her a year or more to work in and through if she was to re-vision our prospect. Reading a long poem by Fitzgerald first takes an effort to understand the method whereby it was composed. Such reading will take effort and time and commitment — effort commensurate, perhaps, with the devotion that went into its composition. To write such a poem it is not enough to have a half-hour after clearing away the dishes after dinner every second night. Maybe this is the reason for the anecdotal poets' displeasure when her name was mentioned.

In the 1970s, when Toronto's Coach House Press was the home for serious innovative poetry, I read everything they published, and in 1975 I read a little book called *Victory*, named after a famous strip joint. It was by a new hotshot poet named Fitzgerald, and it was the real stuff.

Judith had lived a lot of her childhood in foster homes and worse, but in her poems she did not offer us boastful confessions. She was more interested in language than in herself, and she won my heart and brain. For a while she tried being an academic in northern Ontario, but wound up trying to stay alive as a poet on a diet.

During her career, which should have been a lot longer, she produced a series of books that should make us proud that she was one of us. The poems kept getting better and better while her health and luck got worse. Terrible things happened to her, but she did not use them to make people more interested in her. She was a true poet, true to the language that she respected.

Some of her poems got very hard to understand, but they led the way to the kind of beauty that a mathematician or composer works toward. The easy to read Leonard Cohen and the somewhat more difficult Daphne Marlatt were two of her supporters, and while you read their work, perhaps you will know what we are missing.

The book that she called her last was published just before she left us, and the prizegivers ignored it, as usually happens with the best poetry.

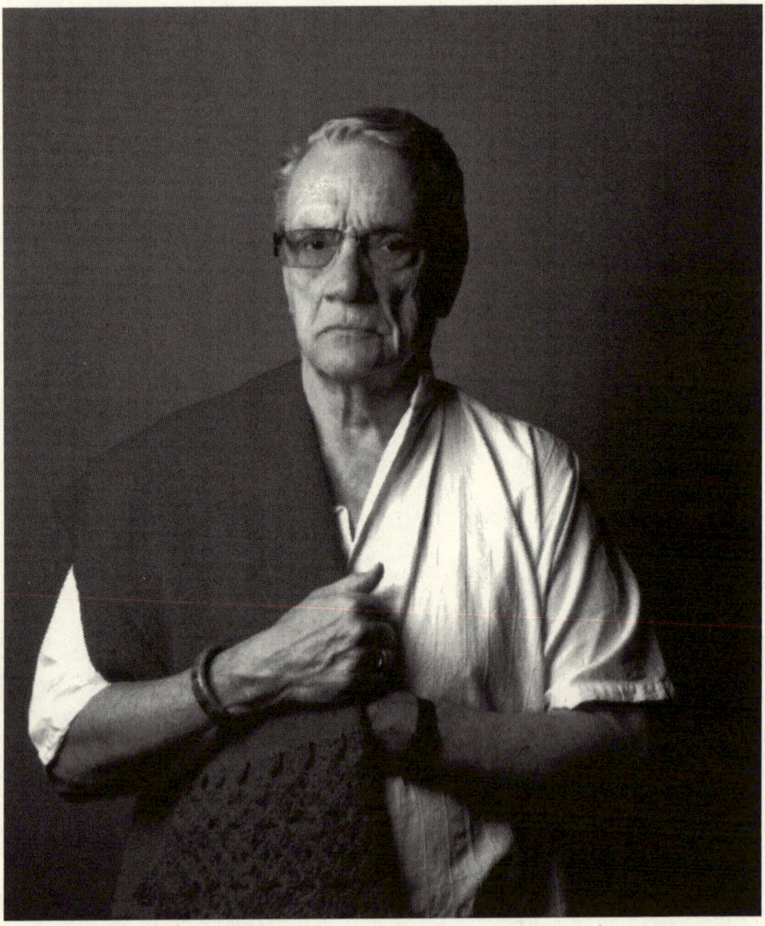

Look at That

Look at that photograph. Look at that man in the photograph. Well, there isn't one. You are looking at a small two-dimensional something. You remember looking at an illustration in a culture magazine and saying to yourself, yes, that is Curnoe. But is it? Isn't it a magazine illustration of a painting that was painted years ago by Greg Curnoe? So when you look at that photograph of the guy with a red shawl over his shoulder, some sort of imaginative power lets you make him adopt the right size and appear in three dimensions. Again — really? In our three-dimensional world, so-called, we see one side of anything. We get used to ascribing reality to that.

Then we try to represent that reality, to use a verb that Henry James thought would do the job here. Call it realism. Realism, I have thought since I turned twenty-one, is an admission of defeat. Whether a landscape or a kaleidoscape, it is an admission of failure. Sometimes a really likeable one, as in *Each Man's Son*.

I have heard of great novels being called the "canon of representation." But isn't that kind of poormouthing a created art? The great quartets of Beethoven and Coltrane don't represent anything (except the body of work managed by those geniuses). I am saying that word "representation" doesn't properly refer to the art work; it refers to what the artist is doing, not so much on canvas or keyboard as in being oneself, maybe an advocate for presentation. Oh no, not again.

Because the referential act leaves out too much. Do you know what I mean? Too much that we do not want to slip away. I want to make it all cohere, like a fuzzy magnet. I am impatient with reference, with continuity, with unity, with the final coming to rest. Morse Peckham called his version of impatience a rage for chaos. I don't think there is any such place. I'm the witch of And/Or.

Thus I have never been able to understand all those Canadian poets and fiction writers and especially professor anthologists who want to trace our literature to explorers' journals. There are so many purposes for setting down words — why assume that frozen John Franklin is a model for you or me?

All right, I have strayed from that image of the old poet with the red rebozo over his shoulder. The photograph is by Alex Waterhouse-Hayward. What I have almost been saying is that I want to write fiction the way he photographs that rebozo. You see, it is an important item of family material. All my life I have been offered stories that treat such items as "symbolic." Not interested. For Alex it is an object that keeps showing up. Its reappearance is as pleasurable and meaningless as the alphabet. I love that. As soon as you start saying things about family heritage and matrilineal blah blah blah I am out of here.

But I should go back and make a little concession. Realism does not have to apologize for being around or for being a downer, as it so often is. Nor do other attempts to convey the real. That shawl looks very real, what with its colour especially, and I might even look convincingly like a Latin American uncle. But I did not feel any rush of recognition when I put it over my shoulder.

Hooray, Difficulty!

As soon as I get up in the morning I sit down and read a few pages of poetry. Sometimes I read poetry that runs on the tracks and offers up the kind of enjoyment you get from the familiar or easy. An example from recent times would be *Where Water Comes Together with Other Water* by Raymond Carver. Good poems with some quirky moments, I would say. Probably more often I will be reading harder stuff, such as the book I am halfway through now, *Charenton*, by Chus Pato, as translated by Erín Moure, a book I first read about five years ago. It is difficult to read. But I have spent a lifetime reading books that are difficult to read. Let's use the U word. I have all my life persisted in reading poetry and prose that I don't understand.

While hanging out in airports or waiting rooms I have noticed that most people want to be understanding what they are reading. Clive Cussler instead of Parmenides, let's say. Let us not say anything about those disturbing people who sit in the dentist's waiting room staring straight ahead for half an hour. Yesterday I thought about those people enjoying their familiar formula novels while their 737B finds its way to Puerto Vallarta. They are a lot like sports fans, I thought. The Brit and the Italian want to watch that soccer game, and can't sit still for baseball. Ontario guys like the comfort and expectedness of ice hockey, and don't have patience for the drowse of cricket.

But during Gertrude Stein's famous tour of the United States in 1934, she attended a college football game and on several occasions compared the experience with the experiencing of art. In a radio interview about her unusual opera *Four Saints in Three Acts*, the interviewer brought up the question of whether any operagoers would understand the work. Stein replied with her usual calm.

"What do you mean, of course they understand or they would not listen to it . . . If you go to a football game you don't have to understand it in any way except the football way and all you have to do with *Four Saints* is to enjoy it in the *Four Saints* way which is the way I am, otherwise I would not have written it that way . . . If you enjoy it you understand it." Then when she talked about the substitutes jiggling on the sidelines, the interviewer said, "But those jiggles are just warming-up exercises." To which Miss Stein replied that it didn't matter what they are doing it for.

But even today, when I am an old coot in the literature business, I get uneasy around poetry that is hard to follow. I see young people writing poems the way the Language Poets write, and ask myself why I come up hard against the materiality of their words. Then I remember the summer when I was twenty-four. I had a job pulling weeds during the hot sunny days, and I spent the evenings reading *Ulysses*. Here is another book I read that summer: *The Lovely Lady* by D.H. Lawrence. What a relief that was! Around that time I was baffled by Pound's *Cantos* but I knew that I should spend the rest of my life reading them. All it took to "understand" them was to make the effort to look up things. But all the while the reader was noticing Pound's wonderful masonry, enjoying the 750-page poem in the *Cantos* way.

    I remember that one day a person who is closely related to me in a maternal way told me that she doesn't want to read anything that was difficult at night because life had given her enough difficulty during the day. And this is a woman who has been in an airport only a handful of times. I think about her and I consider that I have grown old enough to give up the difficult books and enjoy a nice read. So I have made a deal. After I re-read a hundred pages of Louis Zukofsky, I get to snuggle up with William Deverell, who is a very good writer, by the way.

Notes on "I Like Summer"

    I like summer so much,
the way the tiniest rock gets a shadow behind it,
the kind of shadow that makes Mars photographs
    so interesting,
the rocks and shadows you never thought of
when you were a boy imagining a voyage to Mars
or other planets you preferred
because the general run of boys your age were Mars fans
the way they were Roy Rogers fans so you were a
    Gene Autry fan,
and a Red Sox fan because they knew no better than
to favour the New York Yankees, and that continues
so that now young women visiting from Japan
wear pink hats with white New York Yankees insignia
and their boyfriends have their hair dyed blond,
but that doesn't really work because Japanese hair
seems to go orange when you dye it, which is fashion,
isn't it? You have to hand it to someone
who makes an asset out of what looks like a drawback,
hence the invention of scrapple, which I tasted for the
    first time
at the Florida Avenue Grill in Washington, DC,
    having always
wondered what Charlie Parker and Diz were talking
about that winter's night in 1947.

NOTES ON "I LIKE SUMMER"

I was once asked to write a few words about my poem "I Like Summer," wherein I should speak to what's "behind the poem" as well as what I was writing toward, what the influence was, the context or background, and the impetus or spark. I'm sorry to start this so clumsily, but I feel that I have to say something about the difficulty I have in trying to see a relationship between my writing and these notions.

I simply can't tell you anything about what is or was "behind the poem." I know that some teachers used to like to discuss the idea behind the poem or the feeling behind the poem. But honestly, when I am sitting there, pen connecting me with the page, I don't see or imagine anything behind the poem. I am not looking through or around the poem to see something. I don't see any "background"; the poem is immediately present, and any part of it is related not to something elsewhere, but something that is also happening in the poem. Hence rime, for example.

So the only thing I was "writing toward" was the right margin, or the end of the poem. If this poem was otherwise influenced by any specific poet, that would be John Ashbery, whose poems I have been buying since the sixties, and whose work I have been reading in the mornings a lot as time goes by. Yes, I might have been writing like Ashbery, but I think that I do it with a lot more attention to sound. Tone-leading of the vowels, a poet once said.

So a lot of my later poems start with a line that found its way into and through my head: "I like summer so much," for example. Another might have been "I used to wonder what old guys were thinking." Some time later, when I feel the buzz, I will return to the poem and keep adding lines until it is over. "I Like Summer" found its way back, and what a pleasure it is when that happens. And honest to God, I didn't notice till now that the first and last lines are similarly short, and thus have an authority that is the poem's.

How I Wrote *Mirror on the Floor*

Art Imitates Life

The two main characters in *Mirror on the Floor*, George Delsing and Bob Small, are lightly based, as they say, on me and my best friend Bill Lyttle. Get it? Bill Lyttle, Bob Small? I got that idea from Jack Kerouac, who was a big inspiration at the time. Bob and George are also the two main characters in the previous novel I'd written — which was over 500 pages long and too bad to publish — and they show up in later novels and some short stories. Bill and I met when we were about ten or eleven, and we're still best friends to this day.

Page-a-Day Habit

This book, like its predecessor, was written while I was a student at UBC, studying English and History, but I was also doing a lot of other things. With some friends I was inventing and running a poetry magazine called *Tish*, writing a weekly column for the paper *The Ubyssey*, acting in plays, tutoring ESL students, working for *The Raven*, UBC's litmag, getting married. It took me four years to write this 160-page novel. I did a thing that Hemingway said to do: when you get to the bottom of the page, stop. I'd write to the bottom of the page — of course this was in the typewriter days, so it would really be the bottom of an actual page — and that would be it for the day. Even if I was in the middle of a sentence. I had very little time! I was studying and doing all those other things. I was also writing a weekly column for my hometown paper, the *Oliver Chronicle*. Oh, and I liked to write four letters a day, and I was writing a lot of lyric poems, and sending them to hopeless magazines all over. But you had to keep your novel alive, so you stopped at the bottom of the page. My buddy Bill Lyttle, with whom I was rooming, even after I got married, used to say "I gotta know what's happening!" And I'd say "Find out tomorrow night!"

Calm, Cool and Collected

I was just remembering the moment when I found out that the book would be published. I had sent the typescript to McClelland & Stewart because they called themselves "The Canadian Publishers." I just sent it unsolicited. We were having guests for dinner, but I picked up the ringing phone, and it was McClelland & Stewart. They called me in the evening and we were way out west in Calgary, so some editor must have been working really late. They told me they were going to publish it and I very calmly said "Thank you." Then I hung up, jumped up in the air and clicked my heels, and ate my dessert.

Underground Scene

In those UBC times I was living in a different basement every year. That's the way it used to be when you were a student. So I was living in a series of rooms in West Point

Grey in Vancouver — which is where I live at the time of this writing, as they say. But I've moved on up to the above-ground part of the neighbourhood! Anyway, what I always did was to put my little table and my typewriter right at the window, which was always up in a concrete wall. It's not as if I had much of a view; I could see shoes and the bottoms of people's legs, but I didn't even want to be distracted by that. I'd take a cardboard box, pull it apart, and cover the window. I'm still like that. The room I write in right now has had the Venetian blinds closed for at least a year.

Pulp Fiction

In 1967, McClelland & Stewart sent four typescripts of fiction to this outfit out in Manitoba that was mainly printing Harlequin books. Mine was one of them, and Margaret Laurence was another author whose book they sent there. Now they all have brown pages, the paper quality was so bad. They were made of bark, basically. But at least *Mirror on the Floor* never fell apart. The one M&S book of mine that fell apart was my volume of poems *Catch* — I think it was held together with grade school paste!

The Playwright Whose Name Rimes with the Title of His Most Famous Play

Before I left Vancouver in the early sixties the young poets were asserting themselves, and there were lots of them, a Newlove, a Gilbert, a Wah, a Copithorne, many etceteras — and I was happy to find myself a place among them, the Reids, the Gadds, the Bromiges and so on.

When I came back to Vancouver in the early seventies I moved contentedly back into the world of the poets, which now included a whole bunch of newer ones. There were a few novelists around, too, and I found enough to do in playing ball, editing magazines and drinking beer with the poets and novelists.

But what was really happening in Vancouver in the seventies was theatre. Of course one was aware that there were a lot of plays being written and produced by young and youngish writers who preferred to write for the stage, but even though I went to the Players' Club after the Cecil closed at night, I never had the sense to hang out with the playwrights.

As far as drama was concerned, I was interested in two things — Beckett and Shakespeare. Maybe a little Shepard. Really stupid. Talonbooks was publishing my stuff, and I knew that they were the best publisher of Canadian drama in the country. There was a damned theatre renaissance here. Maybe a naissance.

Think of it: Sheldon Rosen, Tom Walmsley, John Lazarus, Margaret Hollingsworth, Betty Lambert, George

THE PLAYWRIGHT WHOSE NAME RIMES

Ryga, Ian Weir, Sharon Pollock, Leonard Angel.
Tom Cone.

When Tom Cone gave his off-the-cuff knockout talk to an overflow crowd at the Vancouver Art Gallery on March 8, 2012, I regretted my stupidity in the seventies, and eighties, and nineties. Tom was at the VAG (for whom he had done great service) to receive the city's first ever lifetime achievement award for active devotion to the arts in his community. That there was an overflow crowd was astonishing, as the event was announced a couple of days earlier. It was common knowledge among these grateful friends that Tom's cancer was fighting a hard fighter.

Colin Browne the poet and moviemaker and close friend of Tom Cone the playwright, librettist, musical promoter and impresario, spoke a beautiful encomium. I was sitting behind Tom, and so I saw a beautiful listening head with familiar twisty hair, and I knew that the man was feeling the extremes of happiness and its opposite. Then we were told that Tom was going to get up on the riser and speak.

I thought that he would say two sentences, perhaps, thanking everyone for coming. What we heard was his famous chocolate truffle voice tell the story of his voyage to our city, and then tell my story, tell our story of growing up in the arts culture in Vancouver starting in the sixties. He told about sitting in Warren Tallman's house and listening to our heroes in what we all call the Allen anthology actually speaking to us somewhat younger hopefuls. As Tom hit the exact true details of the imaginative life in this place over the last decades of the twentieth century, I was, as we used to say, blown away. I don't mind saying that I was trying not to let people see

41

my tears, and I was filled to the top with regret. That I did not hang out with Tom Cone through to the end of that awful century.

But I am also tremendously grateful that I could be his friend in the twenty-first. What ample joy to sit on a couch or the floor at the new music hall known as the Ontario Street house of Karen Matthews and Tom Cone, and hear what the avant garde is doing in Vancouver these years. What pleasurable envy filled my chest cavity when Tom told me about his father's being the part owner of a Single A professional baseball team in Florida. Sure, I know that Tom wrote stuff that got onto the stage in New York City, but baseball, eh? Then how neat that Tom gave me a copy of *True Mummy*, the farthest out you are going to get in Vancouver stage writing.

I will even forgive him for co-writing a hockey opera (*Game Misconduct*) instead of a baseball opera. I understand that ordinary pop culture seeps its way into the arts. Or let me put that a better way: I am pleased to see an excellent writer raise hockey culture up through myth into the mystery of true art.

Yes, I am delighted to be a Conehead in this century. I wish that I had hung around with him in the eighties. Hell, I wish I had been his pal when he was a Florida kid a long time before that.

Well, Rosenblatt

Some years ago at a university on a rainy hill in Burnaby there was a big literature conference on a theme that university professors close to poets thought was nifty. Can't remember exactly. But some of the main panels and so on transpired in one of those big classrooms that look like a movie theatre with writing surfaces attached to the chairs. During one of the serious events a student asked me, "Who is that grumpy old guy stomping back and forth back there?" I looked around, then climbed out of my seat to get a better look. Sure enough, it was Joe Rosenblatt, dressed in ominous attire, doing some of the loudest mumbling you have ever heard, in a language you would leap to associate with deep-sea mammals.

    The foregoing is a description of my late friend Joe Rosenblatt's position vis-à-vis the learned approach to contemporary Canadian literature.

    Joe was born, I imagined, in the late nineteenth century in Toronto, Ontario, and brought up in the fabled Kensington Market of that city's downtown. In his brilliant memoir *Escape from the Glue Factory*, Joe misdirects us expertly and in a very funny prose about the course of his childhood and youth there. It is filled with memorable, and you would say improbable, characters, the one you are likely to remember best being Uncle Nathan. Uncle Nathan "reigned over a fish emporium on Baldwin Street ... His dark fish tanks contained meditative creatures of sea and lake who stared vacuously at their closed perimeters before lapsing into a partial comatose state."

Remember that scene when you consider Joe's decision to live his decades and decades of declining life across the road from the ocean in mid Vancouver Island. On Vancouver Island he joined a number of immodest poets, including Kevin Roberts, Mike Matthews, Ron Smith and Patrick Lane, each of whom claimed to be the best fisherman ever cast ashore by CanLit. I have heard that even Uncle Nathan's fish would have been safe from this particular angler. One of his lyric rivals told me of a time when Joe's fishing line was wrapped numerous times around the boat's waist, something that not even Ernest Hemingway ever saw.

In any case we don't care whether Joe caught many fish in ocean or stream. He brought back a lot of tasty poems. Consider "Bed and Breakfast" from the fishbook *Brides of the Stream:*

> Lured into a dream
> I disrobe in a spotted livingroom,
> stir dark waters, my darker friend
> hieroglyphics lurch across the floor
> to form their cryptic lines for a menu.
>
> There are holes in that quick stream
> where each lair for rent on route
> offers bed and breakfast. This morning
> I wooed a blue tailed lady.

Nobody knows how an inner city kid with a bit of Kipling in his imperial schools ever got to writing and publishing poetry. The usual line is that the thirty-year-old Rosenblatt was "mentored" (to use that creative writing term) by the somewhat more senior Al Purdy and Milton Acorn, and to some extent Earle Birney. Good poets and mentors all, but they championed a poetry growing out of reality. In later years, Joe would have this to say about that: "The very thought of reality gives me hives."

His real companion in the Toronto years was Gwen MacEwen, who lived among old painted boards but wrote about ancient Egyptian magicians with the same gold-flecked kohl around their eyes that she wore. Gwen was a vulnerable and imaginative poet, and the perfect companion for the young Rosenblatt, who prized invention while Souster-like poets around him were making snapshots.

So of course his first book *The LSD Leacock* was published by Coach House Press in 1966. This was the period in which Coach House liked to use magenta ink on tangerine paper in books that snapped apart when you opened them. Someone has stolen my copy of *The LSD Leacock*. I suspect Joe.

Pretty soon Rosenblatt's poetry was full of birds and insects and exotic animals — sort of like his paintings of a later period. By the 1970s his nervous-making drawings or sketches began to invade the books. They had to share space with a poem that thinks you can refer to a simple potato as a "spud messiah." Okay, you get an "organic tub," a bathtub with reptilian feet, containing a couple of dreadfully fat people being addressed by a mouse that is standing on its hind legs atop the taps. I think.

Consider this little observation from the volume *Dream Craters*. It is called "Half an Egg on the Lawn";

The topless zero is a miniature of my mind
without the bird, the sick enigma
fed on light —

Half an egg on the lawn, haunted
loveless like a vacant motel room.

My nerves want to lie down inside, & sleep.

If you knew Joe at all, you knew that he was kind of bashful. I have heard his sketches and paintings referred to as "naïve." I guess that is an art criticism term. But if you think that he was an innocent, somewhat shy Island boy, you might have been surprised to see him feed a pair of pretty women a couple of martinis and induce them to carry him across the old island highway and into the sea. There swam the eager young master of expressive poetry, meditative, perhaps, but never comatose. There bobbed the ancient bard we will celebrate as the centuries pass by.

Six Answers for Rebecca Tuck, Who Asked about Greg Curnoe and Me

1. In 1966 I moved from the west to London, Ontario, and my writing had to undergo a change, because until then it was based, theoretically and otherwise, on my location, on what I and my friends called locus. Being back east, and away from the ground I understood, I needed something else that would give me direction or a handhold. Well, Greg was all hot about what he called (sometimes with ironic defensiveness) "region." We had many arguments about that: I didn't like "region" because it was a word used by outfits who considered themselves the centre of the world — like Toronto, or the usual university poetry anthologies. Blah blah blah. Well, Greg and I often stayed up till early morning, drinking unforgivably black coffee and talking. We were both interested in jazz, for example, but I had let my jazz connection lapse during my three years in arid Calgary. Greg got me back up to snuff (as did the poet John Sinclair in Detroit), and introduced me to the primary and secondary figures in free jazz (whom I still love), such as Albert Ayler, Roscoe Mitchell and Archie Shepp. He also taught me a lot about art, and more and more our arts tended to resemble one another, especially as I enjoyed a Curnoe-like "literalism" in my composition. I am crazy about every period of Greg's work, and have works from many years on the walls in my house. Of all the Curnoe works I am surrounded by, the greatest is *The Woolworth's Rattle*, which is part of a four-

painting series executed in, I think, 1966.

2. In the front room in Greg's house there was a pretty darn good bookshelf, and it contained books that were also vital to my own life. For example, Ezra Pound's *Cantos* and Charles Olson's *Maximus Poems*. I have no notion whether my own writing was influencing Greg's work. But if I remember rightly, I introduced him to David McFadden, the energetic Hamilton poet, and after that they collaborated on several books, Greg doing the visual work in them. McFadden and I always sprinkled our books of poetry with each other's names, since we first met through the mail in the early sixties. Greg, of course, did several covers for my books. We did not write like one another, but we sure understood each other's brains.

3. I was publishing a poetry magazine called *Imago*, for instance, and every third issue was a little book. When I did one by the brilliant Toronto poet Victor Coleman, Greg did the drawing of Victor for the cover. I introduced Greg to Victor, too. As I have said, there are Curnoe works on the covers of several of my books: the novel *A Short Sad Book*, the book of poems *Blonds on Bikes*, the memoir *The Moustache*, of course, and others. While I was living in London, though I was pretty darn busy, I also worked with Greg at the 20/20 Gallery, where one of our masterly shows was a series of penis drawings by John Boyle. I also worked with Greg on the arts journal *20¢ Magazine*. I drummed with the Nihilist Spasm Band until I was thrown out for keeping time. But I have the great honour of having played guitar with the Nihilist Spasm Band three times since Greg's death. I also worked as Greg's assistant in putting up the ill-fated giant mural at Dorval International Airport

during Expo. And so on.

4. In a lot of my writing, fiction or non-fiction or poetry, I do plenty of research. But in the instance of *The Moustache*, to do so would have been to violate the principles by which the "I remember" book, as invented by Joe Brainard, was formulated. In an "I remember book" what gets written down has to be what virtually unbidden enters the poet's consciousness. So, even if you make a mistake in memory, you have to keep it — though you will likely mention that you have made that mistake, etc. So, you don't edit a book like *The Moustache*, except for typing errors, etc. The same thing applies to my "I remember" book about my parents, *Eggs in There* (2006).

5. Through my life, it seems, best friends and former girlfriends have been dying. Apparently after the poet Red Lane died on my twenty-ninth birthday, I was not talking to people much for a year. When Greg died I flew across the country for his funeral. When I heard that bpNichol had died I continued to play the ball game I was playing. On it goes. But I continued to write. I really can't say how much the writing was part of the grieving. In Greg's case, it would seem that it was at least a major pathway, wouldn't you say? A few years ago Jean Baird and I edited the anthology *The Heart Does Break*, in which well-known writers write their experiences of grieving their loved ones. Readers always tell us how much the book means to them during their own grieving.

6. You know, looking at the surfaces surrounding the machine I am now writing with, I see something that resembles Greg's studio. In fact Jean was just here

making suggestions about clearing space for the much bigger machines that are scheduled to find some space here. Greg's studio was not so much "layered" as it was a delicious chaos. The last time I visited it, Sheila showed me the twisted bicycle that Greg had been riding on his last day. I am so glad that it was still in that place, along with the other bicycles that Greg had collected, along with antique toys, a complete taped record of the Anglo-Argentine war, antique soda pop bottles with the pop still inside them, half-finished art works, such as the famous teepee with images of the NSB members on it, hundreds of jazz and blues records, lacrosse equipment, Big Little Books, a drum kit, brightly painted wooden kitchen chairs, boxing gloves, giant watercolours, colour wheels — and if it was layered, that's only the first layer. There was a cat with no tail somewhere, too. I totally understand Greg's sense of order. You would agree if you could look around the room I am writing this in. I will mention seven things (random number): the teak table that the late Warren Tallman had to pile yellow manuscripts or great deli meats on, and which Allen Ginsberg and Robert Creeley wrote at. A plush Hello Kitty doll (which, come to think of it, Warren Tallman's daughter Karen, who is now a psychologist, gave me recently). Four framed drawings by Greg Curnoe in bright coloured frames. A Hello Kitty Pez dispenser. An enormous pile of cables and mouses and so on from former computers. 300 cassette tapes and 300 CDs, mostly jazz and R&B. A photograph of my daughter Thea when she was one hour old.

 And there you go!

Letter to Peter DeLottinville

Peter DeLottinville, QC
Acquisitions Committee,
Library and Archives Canada

Dear Sir,
    As you have seen above, my name is George Bowering. I am a poet and novelist who also publishes Canadian histories and other non-fiction. I am an officer of the Order of Canada, and was appointed the first Parliamentary Poet Laureate (2002–2004).
    Perhaps more pertinently here, I have the honour of having my literary papers collected at LAC. I consider that more meaningful to me than all the prizes and honours I have received over a pretty long life. If I remember correctly, my first fonds went to the National Library in 1985, and was one of the last batches for which cash was paid, and capital gains averted. After that all my donations were marked as gifts, and I was given a break on my income taxes in the years immediately following. The Bowering fonds is one of the largest at the Library, because I work a lot, and because the last gathering included the paperwork engendered by the Laureate position. Although the Library was receiving a shipment every five years, that gathering has been the most recent — that is, about seven or eight years ago. I have a lot of manuscripts and so on sitting here waiting, including my

handwritten diary that was begun in 1958, the year that I first published in a serious literary journal.

So much for introduction. Of course I am available for a lot more information along these lines, but my main interest at the moment is to learn more about what is happening at the Library, and what we might expect in the future, especially in the area of acquisitions. Part of my interest is personal, of course. My biographer and other people I know about have been visiting my fonds of late. But a great part of my interest is related to my sense of citizenship.

I believe that despite its smallish population, Canada is or can be a great nation. I think that a very significant factor in greatness is a determination on the part of a nation to preserve its documentary heritage. One of the most exhilarating moments of my life was the afternoon I went to the British Museum and saw a page written in ink by Percy Bysshe Shelley. In the same year that I first sent my papers to the National Library I was teaching in Berlin, where I saw a page of music from the hand of J.S. Bach. But I got a thrill, too, when I went to Canada's National Library and encountered a poem in the hand of our wonderful poet Phyllis Webb. There has been a lot of talk lately about digitizing our cultural memory, but no amount of computer replication can offer the sheer excitement of seeing and working with the actual manuscripts. I also think that a scholar will work better when the real stuff is there. My experience with the computer is that we get to an awful lot of data, and amount tends to replace quality. A national archive is by its nature, selective. An archive is also organic, if I may use that term, and obviously ongoing. For that reason, putting a hold on collecting is to depart from the meaning of archives.

So you can imagine how proud I was to be in the stacks of that splendid library. I could by now have my collection in various universities. In fact I did sell some early papers to the library of Queens University, and was tremendously gratified when the LAC acquired them to add to the main collection. How secure I felt! And how proud!

That is why, as I approach the end of my writing career and my life, I am worried by the reports I have heard from the newspapers and elsewhere about the present and future state of our collective memory. Present and future generations are the people who will benefit from growth, yes, but economic growth alone will do nothing for our nation's imagination and spirit. Cultural growth is, I maintain, somewhat more important. This truth is well understood in the nations of Europe. I have heard something about the business life of a few Italian families during the Renaissance, but I have seen the paintings that these people bought, and I thank those families for seeing the necessity of both sides of life.

But what about Canada? When I used to visit the National Library, and when I was the Parliamentary Poet, I was greatly impressed by the care and seriousness of both politicians and civil servants, by their understanding of how important our cultural records are. Part of my wonder was due to my being a country boy from the west allowed to visit what I took to be (excuse me) almost sacred premises. Now, with all the negative stories we have been hearing about the relationship between the present Government and the LAC, I am, I have to say, fearful. Last night, as I was going to sleep, I was visited by a nightmare of my papers (and others) being put into a dumpster.

So my main purpose here is to ask you some questions. I don't mean to put you on the spot. I know that there have been nervous feelings around LAC in the past year or two. It's just that as you are involved with acquisitions, you might be able to tell me some of the things I want (and fear) to know. So I will put a few questions here:

Is there a moratorium on the acquisition of new material, and if there is, how long will it last? That is to say, when will the moratorium come up for review? To put it another way: when can I and other writers who have been stalled expect to have our next deposits accepted, and how long will it take for the appraisals to be finished?

Is the work of writers with existing arrangements subject to that moratorium? Is that why, for example, my work has been stalled? I have not talked about this problem with other writers, but I am assuming that their contributions are frozen too. As a collateral question: is there a chance that our contributions will be frozen at their present condition? That would certainly cause problems for scholars in the future.

Is there a sharp reduction in staff, as we have heard in the newspapers, and will that mean that there are not enough people to process our contributions? I certainly sympathize with the people who have to work with less assistance and in uncertainty about their own longevity.

How does the Library see and/or plan the future regarding the collection of Canadian literary archives? We are living in a time of growing panic among writers, academics and archivists.

LETTER TO PETER DELOTTINVILLE

What provisions are being made for existing holdings? I have known over the years of numerous scholars who have gained access to my manuscripts, etc. Will they find it harder to do so? Is there talk of getting rid of holdings? Or winnowing them? If there is, can we be certain that the writers or their literary executors will be alerted and that they can gather their material and go to a university library? I would hate to come to the end of my life, though, knowing that my legacy is not there in the National Library (LAC).

The beloved Canadian poet James Reaney once said that his idea of Heaven was a great archive. I know what he meant. I would like to be there.

Yours sincerely,
George Bowering

In In the Skin

Ever since Michael Ondaatje came upon the scene, I have been slowed in my reading by his choice of titles. *Coming Through's Laughter* puzzled me until I saw my mistake. Laugh, we have come through, D.H. Lawrence might have said. He was a sick person a lot of the time. In *The English Patient* there is no such person. Nor is there any such thing, inside or outside the earlier book as a single work by Billy the Kid, nothing to be collected. *Handwriting* comes in a typeset edition, which is a good thing and an Ondaatje jest, because his handwriting is pretty well unreadable. So what about *In the Skin of a Lion*?

Sure, there must be a hundred essays let loose in the world by professors and graduate students, telling us about the relationship between the epic of Gilgamesh and the novel about working folks in early twentieth-century Toronto, a city that is a lot prettier now than it was back then. Sure, when you have gone to earth, I will let my hair grow long for your sake, I will wander through the wilderness in the skin of a lion.

But those are the first six words we see when we pick up Ondaatje's book. We see a lion's skin before we see anything else, don't we? It's possible that we picture a male lion, the one with hair grown long, at least around his head. That's not his pride, that mane. His pride will wear him out, procreating. We saw that in a documentary about critters doing it. In this case, the cat's stable, or maybe incapable of wandering.

What you will find inside the skin of a lion, if you have the nerve to make such a search, is a lion. If you do not look around for the words of the epic, that is all you will get to know. It is not necessarily true, though, that Ondaatje was misdirecting you in your simplicity. We have seen too many lion skins flattened on tile floors. We have been fooled too often by men in sharkskin suits. This is not to say that Ondaatje is not a trickster. There was a trick with a knife he spent some time learning. And what do you skin a lion with?

Wait! What's that sound?

It's a raccoon lighting. One dainty monster, that boy.

Stop it!

Start again. This gets easier as you go along. Let us think about a reason for the mourning person to wander the wilderness in the skin of a lion. The king of the jungle, emptied out. Does this mourner with the long crazy person's hair hope to assert his royalty, frighten would-be assailants with his stolen pelt? That's pretty hard to imagine. Is the skin what hunters like to call a trophy? A trophy, as if there was some kind of playoff, and the winner gets a lion's biggest organ instead of a loving cup? (And while we're asking questions, or at least I am, why is that thing called a loving cup?) (We do remember that the lion's share is the whole works, or it used to be.)

We do know that the speaker of the lines in question promises to walk around in the wasteland in a large feline epidermis, and this because someone he presumably loves will have gone under the skin of the earth. You recall the famous sackcloth and ashes, raiment for a mourner in the Old Testament. The forlorn would rip their good clothes to bits, replace them with the material we would save for potatoes, sit down and drop handfuls of ashes onto their heads. They didn't usually wander into the wilderness, however, but made for the temple or some other part of downtown.

Wandering endlessly around the wilderness with a lion's skin over one's own — can you imagine how heavy that thing would be, probably smelly too? So it could be that we are talking about penance here. Walking upright or on all fours, or on one's belly? Well, wandering sounds as if it would happen on foot, though probably not purposefully, not in any straight line. You can wander in search of something, or aimlessly. If you found yourself in the wilderness and saw someone wandering while robed in a lion's outside, what would you think?

That guy must be crazy.

That guy must have lost a bet.

That guy is working off some kind of atonement.

That guy must be mad with grief.

It is not likely that you would think that guy must be an immigrant worker in some dangerous and otherwise unpleasant public construction job.

Another thing: whenever someone, a filmmaker, for example, wants to portray the mixed majesty and scariness of the beast, he will present the lion's roaring. But if a human being, let's say particularly a person carrying out penance or mourning, his long hair inside or under a lion's head, were to issue an attempt at a deep-throated leonine roar, would it not appear pathetic if not downright comical?

Which question brings up a consequent thought. What is that person's purpose in choosing to wander in a lion's ex-coat? Lions, I believe, do not wander. They are to be found near watering holes, whether to rest or to hunt. Watering holes are the rudimentary opposites of wilderness. And if the sad person wants to express grief, and if an animal skin is to be preferred over sackcloth, why not the skin of a creature we do not usually think of as proud and regal? How about a gnu, or perhaps an adolescent hippopotamus?

But perhaps I missed a step here. We are familiar with the spectacle of human beings wearing fur or leather, the former skins of various animals such as foxes and snakes and beavers. I once knew a senior poet who wore a suit fashioned from the former container of a cow. Black leather, of course, is meant to convey feelings of an erotic nature, not the despair of lost and never to be regained love.

Still, if I were out in the wilderness, and I saw a lion's skin approaching, or that I was approaching a lion's skin, I would be alarmed, at least at first. Then I might notice that there is a human wanderer inside it, and if he seemed to be slumping rather than threatening, I would relax somewhat — though the fact that this looked like a demented creature would probably keep me on my toes. I may even be made wary due to the fact that the creature is either silent or at most whimpering, rather than roaring. If I were feeling skittish I might even offer a roar of my own. I have been known to offer up such David McFaddeny japes.

Of course, one thing that readers notice about Ondaatje's title is its rhythm. Dah di dah di di Dah dah. Oh the death of a salesman. It's not iambic like *The Man with Seven Toes*. It's not anapestic like *Running in the Family* (well, sorta). If you don't think that Ondaatje thinks of these things, you haven't remembered that he is a poet writing a novel bit by bit. He is not supplying a script for a movie (though he has always been interested in film). Like Margaret Atwood, he is a victim when it comes to movie adaptations.

But remember that Michael Ondaatje learned early to be a trickster when it came to names and titles. His own surname, remember, is a reminder that all names were once (or more often) invented. Invention, it seems, has long been running in his family. You should know enough not to count on the man with seven toes. That guy hopping up and down in front of the locked men's room door? Chances are he's doing the elimination dance.

So Mike and you know that somewhere in some professor's head these words are appearing: in in the skin.

He's Up Again!

Judith Fitzgerald, December 8, 2010: "A month or so ago I received an e-mail from author, editor, and founder of the Al Purdy A-Frame trust, Jean Baird, who could hardly tappy-tip straight, she was so excited. (I kid you not.)

"Reading between the lines between the lines, I gathered she'd snagged a pair of tickets to see Leonard Cohen in concert as a gift for her husband's 75th birthday (although George Bowering was already 75+ 1 day when the concert would take place, December 2nd @ Rogers Arena in Vancouver, but still . . . what a gift! Natch, I shamelessly put both of them to work inmediatamente and requested that the pair write a review of one of the last shows on what I've taken to calling The Never-Ending Tour (which, after an astonishing 247 concerts around the world in two years, concludes Dec. 11 @ the Coliseum in Las Vegas.) Forever (I hope 'n' pray.)

"Natch, they didn't exactly jump all over the idea; but that didn't stop me. (As if!) After the concert there were me me me ipso-quicko in their Mailboxes again: 'Fork it over . . . or else!'

"George buckled first:"

George Bowering, December 3, 2010: "Mr. Cohen went from 8:10 till 11:35 last night, with a break in the middle. The guy amazes all the reviewers with his stamina. I mean, 240 or so of these shows? Jean said I wouldn't be able to get up off my knees half that often, if at all.

Wow!

"My first impression, as we got there an hour early to soak up the experience? I have never been at a musical show where so many people there to be the audience were getting around with canes! I should have brought mine. I saw people with walkers! I also forgot to wear my Order of the Unfried [Unified — Ed.] Heart pin. Damn! Anyway, even though I had to go and pee a lot of the time, I really dug this. Whew! You should have seen that nose on the jumbo screen! This was only my second ever music show at a hockey rink, the earlier one being decades ago, when I saw Cream at a rink in Calgary. I am glad to have added it to my life's experience. Sad that in three hours they didn't do my favourite song, 'Famous Blue Raincoat,' but I am trying to stop having favourites — that's bad esthetic. Douglas Todd, the religion writer for the *Vancouver Sun*, reviewed the show and praised Leonard, pointing out a few times that this is near the end of the guy's career. I sensed you there, sitting with us."

JF, December 8, 2010: "(I was there, in spirit, beaming to beat the bland! 'That's it?' I e-bugged Jean and George. 'That's the entire review? Who did you see? What did he do? How was the performance? Details!'

"George e-blabborated the next morning."

GB, December 5, 2010: "I can cast my head back and say a few things about the LC event. Still remembering all those people with canes. Like everyone else, I am awed by L's energy. I mean, he's older even than I, and he is up and down, back and forth, and after 3.5 hours, as you predicted, he skipped off the stage."

JF: "Told ya so! :)! Next time someone addresses THE Boss. they can call him Skipper. Go on . . ."

GB: "The band is very tight and interesting. The mixture of instruments is a pop, I mean, on top, I mean, of what I kept hearing as a blues frame, despite the bandurrias and waltzes. And then those two sisters [the Webb Sisters], in the very middle of one song, perform side-by-side cartwheels! While the master grins. LC is a nice subtle actor, and, you know, I am persuaded that he is dumbfounded by his own success, that he appreciates it. He is never above the crowd. And you know — he CAN play a guitar better than you would think. I do remember that he had a country-and-western band, the Buckskin Boys, at McGill. Don't let anyone tell you Leonard Cohen didn't have a sense of humour.

"The audience was with him. They weren't just leaning their chins on their canes. You knew that they know all the songs, have them at home on vinyl, recognize all the opening hooks. You know which song got the biggest roar and handclapping from all those geezers? 'Closing Time.'

"Jean and I were pretty close, Row 12 in the hockey seats, stage left side. Jean wouldn't have been able to throw skivvies that far. We were under one of the high TV back-projected screens, and I have to tell you — during close-ups that is one scary nose!

"Huh! Jean was paying attention! This was a happy crowd. A lot of people had to do something next day, but no one left after the first 1.5 hours, when the break happened. A lot of those people in the hockey building looked like squares — you know, your Mum and Dad's friends in whatever small town; but they knew what was happening up there. As I said, I had only once before been to a big pop music show in an arena. I loved it. I felt old and Canadian and poetical.

"It was, I know for a fact. good for me. 'Good for you,' I said to the poet in the suit."

JF: "That afternoon? Jean ups the ante in what the Skipper calls the Holy Game of Poker."

Jean Baird, December 5, 2010: "Many years ago, I was blessed to hear Alberta Hunter [one of Skipper's faves!] at the Cookery in NYC. She was, and in my mind still is, one of the most sensual women I have ever seen. She was in her eighties at the time. A decade or so later, I heard Yehudi Menuhin in Lewistown, NY. He had an escort at each elbow to get him onstage. He was frail, but once he put that violin under his chin, he was transformed. Me too. George and I went to a concert in Vancouver by Ornette Coleman, and a year later one by Sonny Rollins. Coleman was 78, Rollins was 79. But both completed two-hour sets without once sitting down. How do they do that?

"The 8000+ sellout audience in Vancouver greeted Leonard Cohen's entrance, complete with his trademark Brooks Brothers Suit and fedora, with a standing ovation. [Some were slow standing up with canes.] Cohen began with "Dance Me to the End of Love," bent down on his knees, singing to the virtuoso bandurria player from Barcelona, Javier Mas. I repeat, on his knees. I was nervous. I mean, most folks that age go out of their way to avoid getting down on their knees. But then Cohen gracefully stood. I didn't count the number of times, but in the first set he was down on one or both knees over and over again. Then he announced a break and skipped off the stage, waving over his shoulder. Ornette and Sonny have nothing on Leonard.

"It was that sort of night.

"It seems that Cohen has always been part of my life. 'Suzanne' was a hit the year I was ten. My kids knew all the songs from car trips. Like many others', Cohen's poetry is part of the fabric of my life. Years ago, because of my art and literature magazine that published work by teens, I did a lot of public speaking about the importance of creativity in our lives. One of my favourite parlour tricks was to begin, let's say, a presentation to a Rotary group by announcing that we were going to have a short poetry contest because I knew they were all big poetry fans and experts. I always got the expected nervous groan. 'I'll give you two lines, and you have to give me the name of the poet.' They all knew Leonard Cohen, and the trick made them realize that they were poetry fans.

"And that's what most impressed me about the concert, that Cohen several times drew away from the music, reciting the poetry, reminding us about language and its power. Cohen shows such deep respect for that power.

"On the way home in the car I asked George how many children he thought that man is responsible for. George said he wasn't sure how many children Cohen had. No, I said, that's not what I meant."

My Heart in Hiding

When I was in high school my favourite serious poets were Dylan Thomas and Hart Crane. Young people ought to read Dylan Thomas and let him swarm all over them. In later years they will probably think that they have outgrown him. As for Hart Crane — when I was a high school kid I had no idea how difficult Crane was. But I was fascinated by what he did on the page with the faltering airplane section of *The Bridge*.

There have been a lot of poems that turned out to be important gates in the pathway of my life, and all of them offered better metaphors than the one you have just read. After three years in the air force, I went to the University of British Columbia, and decided to read all the poetry in the PS section of the library. PS stands for US literature. I was reading alphabetically, because I could not think of a better way to find what I was looking for. It took a while to get to W, of course, but eventually I found a quite newly published book called *The Desert Music* by William Carlos Williams. The title poem was so hot that the book dropped from my hands and made a loud splat on the concrete floor. From then on William Carlos Williams would be my poetry Dad. I'm happy about that. I'd never get to W if I were starting now.

Even while I was a UBC student, my friends and I made some kind of fuss across the country with our poetry newsletter *Tish*, and our championing of the new

USAmerican poets that were unknown to our professors. They provided poems that would always stay with me and my poetry buddies, poems such as Robert Duncan's "Poem Beginning with a Line from Pindar," and Charles Olson's "Songs of Maximus" and Robert Creeley's "The Door."

These poets, who would later be called "post-modern," sprang from various traditions, including a certain US tradition of modernists, mainly Williams and Ezra Pound. For me and my buddies, hardly a day went by when we would not read or talk about Pound's translation of Cavalcanti's "*Donna mi prega*." I was particularly taken with the early Imagist poems of H.D., and later I would fall upon her wartime *Trilogy* and find the great long poem of my life. I was very proud that it had been printed originally by the Bowering Press of Plymouth.

So we were very hip young poets, the newest avant garde, rising out of the ocean's edge to frighten the poetry old folks of eastern Canada.

But we learned things in our actual classrooms from time to time. It was in one of those classrooms that we came upon a poem that soon we would all go around reciting. Would it surprise you to know that the poem is a sonnet? More than that, it is a Christian sonnet. More than that, it is a nineteenth-century Christian sonnet written by an Englishman!

I am talking about Gerard Manley Hopkins's "The Windhover."

Our attraction to this poem was normal, I guess. Hopkins was so avant garde that the poem was not published till 1918, twenty-nine years after the poet's death. His poems are extravagantly vocal, and just jammed with images. Here we were, a bunch of young university poets desperate to be anti-academic; and for us, followers of Olson and Duncan and Allen Ginsberg, this meant the poem as spoken, and the poem as images. We were also into theorizing about poetics and composition (for which we would always be derided by the "natural" poets back east), and Gerard Manley Hopkins wrote some of the greatest compositional theory of all time. It was there in our beloved Penguin paperback of Hopkins's poems. You could look it up.

Hopkins wrote Christian sonnets because he was a monk, and thus willing to serve discipline and order. But he was an ecstatic, and needed to discover ways to burst into praise for earthly beauty. The normal tight discursive Miltonic sonnet could not hold his heart and his breath, so he found ways to stretch the lines and make the meter soar. Like a bird, maybe. Like a beautiful rebel. Yes, he was a monk, and monks are supposed to be humble and colourless. But what if your subject was God's grandeur or pied beauty. Dazzling and delicious nature are signs of God's care, and a puny poetics would never do it justice.

This is the way a Robert Frost sonnet starts:

I have been one acquainted with the night.
I have walked out in rain — and back in rain.

Already the reader knows better than to expect any soaring. It's going to be all measured walking, probably with a period at the end of the line.

Compare the first two lines of the Hopkins poem. It makes the Frost poem sound like prose written by a sleepy person. Imagine the nerve — to say "morning" twice in a row, to have three M-words followed by six D-words, to have twenty-six syllables (and a bit) where you are supposed to have twenty. God, we used to have fun trying to recite these lines, trying to remember "daylight's dauphin, dapple-dawndrawn."

You couldn't help getting it a little wrong from time to time. When the young poet David Dawson and I saw each other on campus, we would wave and shout, "Hi there in your riding!"

You would never get away with something like that in an English class, but I still think it was part of learning to like and respect a great poem.

One of the things about reading Gerard Manley Hopkins was that you had to look up a lot of words, either because they were old fashioned or because you weren't old enough to have them in your vocabulary yet. So you would find out that "wimple" is that accordionated white fringe on the front of a nun's head gear. Or that "sillion" is a furrow in the farm earth. Or that "buckle" means fold up but also refers to the use of the short sword that a knight holds in his left hand while he's swinging away with his regular sword in his right hand.

That's another enjoyable thing about Hopkins's poetry, that while the sound is very lush, the poem is also packed to the bursting point with images. In these fourteen (well, fourteen-plus) lines, Jesus is a windhover, all right, a hawk in the breeze, but he is also a knight, a chevalier, so there's horse stuff. The "dauphin" rimes with "Falcon," but the Dauphin is the French king's knightly son, just as Jesus is God's son. You could find out why the French called this prince the Dauphin, etc. Hopkins, of course, knew. But there is also ice-skating, soil-plowing, and eventually the Easter passion of Jesus. There are a million things. I will just show you a bit about the Easter stuff, as it appears in the last line.

The words that tip you off? They rime, to start with, and that is what rime is for, to make connections that will work in other ways than just sound. The words here are "fall," and "gall" and "gash." They tell the details of Jesus's sacrifice, his falling while he carried his cross to the hill, the vinegar that was given to him when he asked for water, and the hole made in his side by a Roman's spear. But at the same time these words are descriptive of the burnt firewood (I have always imagined a fireplace) that all at once falls and breaks open to reveal the bright burning inside.

That's the direction Hopkins has been heading all through the poem. The windhover, he says, is masterful when it rides the wind. He says that it is in "ecstasy," which means escaping stasis. But it is more beautiful when it folds its wings and dives, presumably after its prey. Hopkins was a Jesuit, and the Jesuits liked the idea of Jesus's pursuing human beings rather than just asking them to follow him. He is usually pictured as a warrior knight complete with horse and sword and buckler. Just so, the dogged working of a plow turns the earth and makes it shine.

The story of Jesus is the story of a heavenly Son who falls to earth voluntarily, all the way to earth and inside it. Hopkins says that there is the real beauty in his religion.

That is a bare outline of Hopkins's poem, maybe a hundredth of the details and ambiguities that make it, really, one of the longest poems in the English language. Any reader is welcome and encouraged to ask lots of questions. What is it about the scraping a skate's heel does as the skater makes a tight turn? Why is the poet's heart in hiding: is he a rabbit waiting for those talons? Aren't there a lot of sharp things in this poem — talons, skates, spears, swords, plows? Gold vermilion: those are the traditional colours of British kings, aren't they?

Why does Hopkins use only two end-sounds in the first eight lines and only two more in the last six lines? And why does he use a one-syllable sound and a two-syllable sound in either case? Hmm, I said when I was about twenty. Hmm, I still say, even now when I know what "sillion" means, and remember that both falcons and knights wear plumes — and that poets write with them.

See, what I am saying is that such a poem is so much fun, partly because it is so lovely-sounding, and partly because it compresses so many images and implications. It is the kind of poem that will last you all your life. Another good example is Shelley's "Ode to the West Wind," maybe the simplest-sounding, most complicated poem in the English language.

There are some poems that you like all your life for their startling simplicity and clarity. William Carlos Williams wrote a lot of those. But I will tell you something about a poem like "The Windhover." Decades and decades after you read it for the first time, you can sit down somewhere and open the book and read that poem, and all at once get one of those "Aha!" experiences that the best poems save up for you all through the years.

Did you notice that Hopkins specified "shéer plód"? Those two down-beats sound a lot like stomping, don't they? The phrase also rimes with the line "Generations have trod, have trod, have trod" from another sonnet, "God's Grandeur." Hopkins was always doing that, too.

I am not going to perform a critical reading of "The Windhover," as they say. I would not be satisfied that I had made a start until I had burned up fifty pages. But I would like to say this: I am really glad that three decades after his death, Hopkins's poems were published by some people who did not want them to be kept from the world any longer. Thank you, as I often find myself saying to editors and other monks.

He Gets Better Every Year

"D didn't seem to have any morals at all, except where phrasing was concerned." So wrote David Bromige about an unashamedly autobiographical figure he spoke for in *Piccolo Mondo*, a comic novel he co-wrote with us other three initials A, G and M. I remember Bromige's phrasing very well as one of the first things I noticed about him when we were students at the University of British Columbia in the late fifties and early sixties.

In those days there were a lot of professors from the USA at UBC, many of whom were escaping the California loyalty oath. At the same time, there were a lot of Brits among the faculty of arts students, a lot of them named Anthony. These people took over the arty segment of the campus newspaper, the year-end annual, the players' club and all other manifestations of arty-fartiness. A star among them was David Bromige, recently arrived from his job as a nurse in a loony bin in Saskatchewan, or so it was rumoured. It was also rumoured that he had come to Canada as a draft-dodger during the Suez crisis.

As the years went by, and Bromige became my friend, I learned the bare outlines of his younger life (he was 2.5 years older than I, but not according to his story). Some things I learned were fictional but always phrased in an interesting way. He was born in London just in time to be a boy in the Blitz, about the time when I was living in an Okanagan orchard, not quite yet learning to grow my animosity for the Brits who would move in and take over my little town and environs.

I don't think that David was thinking of taking over a Canadian orchard when he enrolled at the Berkshire College of Agriculture a few miles from the town in which my grandfather sold newspapers as a boy. David proved to be ill-suited for complex modern farm operations such as driving a tractor, so he dropped the academic approach to agriculture, and went to work on a dairy farm in Sweden. I think that the biography at this point takes on the advantages provided by fiction and poetry.

Anyway, Sweden's loss became Canada's gain when David found his way to the Canadian prairie around the time that I was an air force photographer there (incidentally, having an appendix operation that kept me from doing my part in the Suez crisis). I still like the loony bin story, though in the photograph we have of David on the prairie, he does look kind of agricultural. Probably you would say that going from nut-house nurse to UBC undergraduate was a lateral move.

David arrived during an interesting time. Soon two new official literary journals began there — George Woodcock's *Canadian Literature*, a non-stodgy critical mag, and *Prism*, which was connected with the new creative writing program. The traditional student mags were *The Raven*, which was known mainly for its daring design, and a satirical rag no one remembers. There was a lot of theatre, some of it Brecht and some of it original student plays. Art Pepper and Lee Konitz came to play for us. All this stuff got reviewed and analyzed in the arts pages of *The Ubyssey*, edited by David Bromige.

But what poets came to read on campus? Why, those

respected by the squares who ran the English department: George Barker, Marianne Moore, Stephen Spender, W.D. Snodgrass. UBC's magazines were full of people who wrote poems like theirs.

On the other side of campus there were youngsters who were reading poets that only two of their professors (Ellen and Warren Tallman) knew about — contrarians such as Charles Olson and LeRoi Jones. And when, late in 1959, their bible, Donald Allen's *The New American Poetry, 1945–1960* arrived, the poetry wars were on. Ellen Tallman knew the poets in San Francisco, and Warren Tallman came up with the outrageous notion of pooling our scant money to bring Robert Duncan on a Greyhound bus to tell us what could happen in poetry, like after T.S. Eliot.

Now we had two mutually exclusive poetries going, especially after the upstarts, with the prodding of their hero Duncan, started their monthly mimeographed poetry "newsletter" *Tish*. The title had been half-laughingly supplied by Duncan as a tribute to his teacher Ernst Kantorowicz, who'd pointed out that while the oldest agricultural traditions in the world used human dung as fertilizer, the Anglos and their offspring flush it into the ocean. *Tish* as a title also reminded us of Duncan's talks about rime, one of whose variants is phonetic inversion. Of course the inattentive poetry drones would continuously maintain that *tish* is *shit* spelled backward.

I was the only person I knew who spent time on both sides of the campus — with Tishers Frank Davey, Fred Wah and Jamie Reid, and with David Bromige and the Anthonys. I was, I thought, drinking with the enemy. Brom wrote a little poem about my girlfriend's knee, but the one I remember totally is: "Borrowing from Bowering

/ is a neat feat." I just put up with the situation. Bromige would make fun of *Tish* and its brash seriousness, and I would get blasted at parties with Bromige and his friends with their British accents.

And then I don't know what happened. After the famous summer 1963 poetry jamboree at UBC, which featured Ginsberg, Olson, Levertov, Creeley, Avison and Duncan as teachers, I left town. A year or so later, I heard that David Bromige was at Berkeley, and learning everything he could from Robert Duncan.

See? Here's what happens. When the Brits get good at language, it usually comes out as wittiness. But ask Robert Duncan what "wit" means, and he will direct you to Sanskrit, where it is at the core of understanding, where "gna" leads to knowledge and "vid" leads to vision. In around 1965, I thought good, Bromige is dropping the English stuff and coming on over.

So, in the next four decades, Bromige became an important part of west coast poetry. He finished up at Berkeley, became a straw-hat academic in California wine country, and wrote book after book of curious phrasing, just what we needed. Sometimes he was grouped with the west coast contingent of the Language Poets, and he certainly took language as his particular job, but he was too restless to stop poking his formidable nose in elsewhere:

>The brief
>lyric poem as we
>have wanted it
>to be for centuries
>here in the west
>gets valorized

again, a neat
relief from far
more complicated
as the Frenchmen say,
*existence (auf Deutsch,
Existenz.)* Beauty
and Truth chased
one another round
and round the vase.

2

Reading or re-reading the hundreds of pages in his posthumous selected volume, *if wants to be the same as is*, I am knocked for a loop. That's my critical response. How often we have tried to peg him, that Brit Canuck Yank songster, while all the time he was making his own door and coming through it. How neat (to use one of his favourite words) to go back and read his first book *The Gathering* (Sumbooks, 1965), and realize that he was always better than you thought he was. He could have been foretelling the problem of the European semioticians in a little poem titled "The Sign." It ends:

I remember

that sign I heard of, reading
Don't throw stones at this sign

David did, so you should consider the autoreferentiality, especially since the memory invoked occurs after the poet's declaration that he "me[a]nt nothing." His clarity produces lovely ambiguity from this moment on, produces a priceless body of verse. I can hear Robert Grenier nodding his head, while the Imagists still among us enjoy the heck out of the references.

In *The Ends of the Earth* (1968) his first Black Sparrow book, which is dedicated to Robert Duncan, Bromige used a page to tell us why he, as did Duncan, spelled words in an unprescribed fashion. Sometimes the explanation is silly, but then he says, "to get a sense of informing accent," and this reader at least is eager to pick up the phone. One recognizes that this early did Mr. Bromige begin to sniff out what Mr. Bernstein would come to call Bent poetics. We are not here to purify the language. Bernstein writes, "A poetics is valuable to the degree that it is able to engender other possibilities in response, both complementary and oppositional." (*Pitch of Poetry*, University of Chicago Press, 2016, p. 297.)

A little difficulty in reading can wake you up. I don't know about you, but I have often had to re-read and sometimes re-re-read to figure out what Bromige's title might mean. It took me months to figure out *A Cast of Tens*, for heaven's sake. *Tiny Courts in a World Without Scales* is at least a poser. *As in T as in Tether* I think I got while reading it a second more attentive time. The aforesaid *if wants to be the same as is* is my favourite when it comes to name double-takes.

TV talk show host: "I found that I had to keep going back and checking what you'd written on an earlier page."

Toni Morrison: "Yes, Dear. That's called reading."

You will remember that Bromige wrote that his character (wrong word, I know) D had no morals whatever except where phrasing was concerned. Getting it exactly true is a duty, a matter of honour, a case of "right" being simultaneously good and precise. And here's the beautiful problem: there were no ten commandments lugged down the hill by some chief linguist. You're up or out there alone, where your simple little quatrain will forever have your best reader baffled, forgetting his lunch, grinning till his heart comes back home:

> The imagination
> . seizes on
> some further
> series of itself

How many times, not to change the subject, have you read the hell out of Shelley's "Mont Blanc" and finally understood it? I've done it twice. Like Shelley, David Bromige is a philosophical poet who would die for beauty while knowing its inadequacy.

3

As a Bromige reader I am delighted by the editors' rescue of *American Testament*. The subject was very important to David, and it is probably why we can hear his multi-inflected voice as we listen, for instance, our way down the columns of "As Long As Purgatory Rimes With Virtue," that graph yes, of a mind we loved so much, moving, riming as it moves, arguing and confessing:

> Yet
> words please us most

>   keenly when strung
>   along a plot that
>   keeps us in suspense
>   and no state known
>   to us is more
>   valuable than
>   happiness.

    A Language Poet can enjoy something on Netflix, but still slice through your lyrical bromides when it needs doing. Have you noticed that Charles Olson paraphrased John Keats, just as surely as William Carlos Williams had? I'm saying that David Bromige did not lose any of his edge when he delivered an image, and he did not lose any of his music when he became post-Deleuzianly philosophical. Somewhere Ron Silliman said that Bromige opened up the question of "language's cognitive domain." Question is right. A poet I know may have been agreeing when she said that Mr. Bromige was disruptive and cuddly, and looked quite a bit like the pictures they show us of Jesus. *American Testament*, indeed.

The Objects of My Affection

At the end of January 2018, while I was working on a new book in Mexico, I got an e-mail from Jack David, publisher of ECW Press, in which he informed me that some of the women at ECW who had read the manuscript of No One *were uneasy with ECW's publishing it, feeling that the fiction "objectifies women." These women, Mr. David told me, work in publicity, marketing, and editorial.*

He did for us all the respectful thing of reading the manuscript again, and because the writing is good, decided to go ahead with printing and publication. But he would not force anyone to work on the book if they felt that it should not be published. Therefore "the result will possibly be less attention for the book."*

So I decided to write the following letter in an attempt to defend my novel.

To some of ECW's workers:

I would feel so much better if I could address you by name, because a conversation works better that way, but I will respect anyone's wish to be anonymous in this regard. If any awkwardness eventuates due to this situation, please understand that I would like a fair exchange of information and views.

As I am in my eighties, and it is unlikely that I will have time to write another novel, I am disappointed. The few women and men who read the manuscript before I submitted it have called it a very good book and my best fiction; I guess I would rather see it attacked by the

---

*A year after its publication, there have been no printed advertisements or reviews of *No One*.

critics than semi-censored before its birth. My publisher has called it "a strong piece of writing — funny at times, caustic, realistic, and surprising." Before starting this conversation with you, I read the book again, and was unshyly impressed with the writing.

First, let me say a few words about objectification. As is my wont, as you know from reading the text, I like to begin with a look at etymology. For my fellow novelist Audrey Thomas, that would mean opening a Skeat; for me it has always been Partridge.

If you are accustomed to using books of word origins this way, you start with "object," and once you get something like the thing thrown out for consideration, you look at "subject," the thing thrown under, and "interject," the thing thrown between, and "eject," the thing thrown out. Of course, this is fun, so you have to make sure you don't just spend the next ten hours turning pages in your Partridge. But you remember that it was long ago that you were a young poet, finding out that etymology was the best ever generator of metaphors (and no, we are not here going into the common discovery that that word has to do with carrying across). And we remember learning that the roots of words are not what happened in the past, but what makes the plant stay alive now.

So, so far, "object" has no negative connotations. What about "objectification"? I guess we have to surmise what is meant by the term, figuring that out by looking at the alternative. I have not yet been instructed as to what the author should do rather than see his characters objectively. One answer would be to treat their experience subjectively. But I have also heard male authors vilified for attempting to write from the point of view of a female character. I don't want to treat any character (or person) as a subject, having an unpleasant memory of being called, in my youth, a "British subject," and a "subject of the Queen/King." Perhaps that is partly why I was attracted to Charles Olson's famous essay "Projective Verse", wherein he suggested using the term "objectism":

> Objectism is the getting rid of the lyrical interference of the individual as ego, of the "subject" and his soul, that peculiar presumption by which western man has interposed himself between what he is as a creature of nature (with certain instructions to carry out) and those other creations of nature which we may, with no derogation, call objects. For a man is himself an object, whatever he may take to be his advantages, the more likely to recognize himself as such the greater his advantages, particularly at that moment that he achieves an humilitas sufficient to make him of use. It comes to this: the use of a man, by himself and thus by others, lies in how he conceives his relation to nature, that force to which he owes his somewhat small existence. If he sprawl, he shall find little to sing but himself, and shall sing, nature has such paradoxical ways, by way of artificial forms outside himself. But if he stays inside himself, if he is contained within his nature as he is participant in the larger force, he will be able to listen, and his hearing through himself will give him secrets objects share.*

*Charles Olson, "Projective Verse", in *Collected Prose*, edited by Donald Allen and Benjamin Friedlander, University of California Press, 1997.

Sorry to go all theoretical on you, but I take these things seriously, and unlike a lot of Canadian writers, I don't just write as if it were a naturally inherited skill.

Here's another problem to discuss: if objectifying is something bad, who is doing it here, the narrator or the author? Or to put it another way, how long does it take a reader to agree with Honey that the narrator is an "asshole"? Or is Honey guilty of objectifying when she calls him that? I have to admit that the accusatory use of that word confuses me. Maybe we should find another term of vilification. This is why I wish that we were in conversation, instead of relying on the hearsay I heard. In not wanting the book to be publicised and distributed, are you hoping to thwart me or my fictional character, whom I do not champion or identify with?

Odysseus is commonly considered the first great hero of (semi)western literature. We don't really know who Homer was, whether he was just one person, whether he was necessarily male as is his creation. We wonder how much the *Odyssey* derived from myth and how much was human poetry. In ancient Greece a hero was a man who had the courage to venture beyond the sight of familiar land. Yet the frame of Odysseus's post-*Iliad* story was his attempt to get back with Penelope and Telemachus. "All I ever wanted to do was get home and be with my wife," avers the narrator of our book on page 5 and pretty often throughout the text. So, he compares in that regard with Homer's hero, and we are invited to compare him as well with Euripides's slayer of the Cyclops, Tennyson's Ulysses, and Joyce's Leopold Bloom. In our conversation, I would be interested to hear your observations in that regard.

Similarly, if you took up my narrator's suggestion

to read the novel *Yesterday, at the Hotel Clarendon*, you will understand why it belongs in my story, and you will have understood my narrator's behaviour in his relationship with that novel's author, Canada's best-known feminist poet and fiction writer. As you know, I have long been a fan of intertextuality, and my bargain with my reader has often, if not usually, involved other texts, from the past or the present. So the lotus-eaters of my novel cannot be seen independently of those in Tennyson's poem and maybe in contrast to Odysseus's Protestant-like self-denial. So you have been invited by the lotus-eaters episode to compare Delsing with the heroic warrior Odysseus. Would you prefer one over the other? I am interested in such notions.

Thus, in the chapter that runs pp. 195–201 you will have enjoyed, perhaps, some important differences between Cissy and the original Circe. I hope you found the treatment funny. In truth, my whole interrogation of the epic won't work if the comedic odour is not always somewhere around. For example, can you imagine our Attic hero's whistling "You're nobody till somebody loves you" as he enters the cave of the one-eyed monster or the bedroom of the swine-rancher?

But also, in the moment of such laughs, you will have noticed, our narrator (as on p. 202, and so often elsewhere) forebears and forbids the famous "male gaze," asking readers to employ their own imaginations if they desire to. He also, as on page 210, says that readers who are annoyed or bored, should skip the following passage. This does not always happen (and there is a reason for that, too) but it happens more than once or twice.

Here is something I wonder about: in reading the text and noting that the narrative resembles an eighteenth-century picaresque, did you pause to think that the allegorical variety of the "hero's" encounters might be accompanied by a sampling of various assertions in recent attacks against fictional portrayals of sexual relations between (or among) the sexes? I began this letter, we remember, with my problem in seeing the presence of "objectification." I tried getting behind some other eyes, but in the first two pages of the book we meet the alleged objectifier, and I, for one, ask whether an objectifier thinks about his "wronging" a woman?

No help there.

All right, then the narrator compares himself with Kirk of the naked thighs, and for the first time invites some chuckles or at least smiles aimed in his direction. Then he is called an "asshole," something his heroic forebear didn't have to hear.

So, let us see the women our adventurer encounters in his mock-epic voyage. I would like to say here that he never denigrates one. In fact, I would venture to say that he feels admiration for all of them. If I were writing a critical article about this quest story, I might take note of the "central figure's" posture in each encounter. Begin as the book does, with Danaë. He has to enter her room on his hands and knees. When he gets there, Danaë throws him around. (That *-ject* root again.) Here we might consider the question of sex and power. It is clear that Danaë wields the power, and that Delsing admires her. I think we are being introduced to a theme here. Even in the scene with Fé, the first one to feature a description of sex, after a hundred pages have gone by, I can't find any imbalance of power.

I think that the baffling question of "objectification" could better be understood as a question of power. There are, in the novel, two scenes in which an often-considered question of power and sex comes up, i.e. when there is a possibility of the teacher's taking advantage of the student by withholding grades or the like. In one instant, he stops the procedure; in the other, he is promised that the student-teacher relationship is over. In the chapter that takes place in the Ivy League, I can see no instance of the male person employing his power. I believe that the main thing that is going on for the writer and reader is the wordplay, the literary allusions and the humour that results. I think it's really funny, and it is therefore my favourite episode in the story. And it is accompanied with the oft-repeated suggestion to the reader to do her own imagining. The narrator helps somewhat, as with his introduction of the word "power" on page 223, followed quickly by his use of the other abstract word "homage." I kind of think the author had this choice in mind when it came to the book's argument.

    Speaking of which, I would be interested to know your reading of the passage (pp. 217ff) about inappropriate stuff and politically correct stuff. You might also go back to page 10 and tell me what you think of the skinny old woman with the violin on the Bayou Teche. Do you think that she is being objectified or admired? Don't you think she takes her place among the women of this book just as she does with the author and characters in the other novel mentioned in her paragraph? The narrator of my novel says that he feels love for these old Louisiana musicians and dancers, love "without a trace of sex in the neighbourhood."

    Remember that this claim is being made by a guy who had been a twenty-one-year-old virgin. The scene in which he recalls the loss of his virginity shows him to have been rather feckless during the event. Concerning his history of extramarital sex, he admits, "most of my adulterous experience had been accidental or marked by shortcomings." Do you think that such an honest admission is likely to be made by a person who wields power over exploited victims? I may be wrong, but I think that he is more often than not a figure of amusement, more of a Tom Jones than a Hugh Hefner. I thought I might clarify things or make them more nicely foggy with my burlesque of the returning hero in that little chapter about Odysseus and Penelope that ends with her calling him a "fucking asshole" (pp. 89–91), wherein both words might be considered.

I also liked indulging myself with clever allusions befitting a modernist writer, eh? In the chapter about initials I prided myself about preparing the story of Z and the Story of O (hence Oz), and then slipping in the remark "re age", which, if the first letter were capitalized and the second letter were pushed to the right, and outfitted with an acute accent, would give us the pen-name for the author of the most famous erotic novel of 1954. Yes, it is my typical indulgence, and complicates the intertextuality and all that, but I don't think I am the only person in this activity who thinks such play is funny even though instructive.

I do not expect all my readers to get all my allusions, heaven forbid. I know better than to hope that they will look up references, to find out, for instance, why my narrator said "I blessed the name Agrestis Nettar Ibleo," though the humour will be diminished and misunderstood if they don't.

Well, in the old days, before Pauline Réage, censorship

was practised or urged for any text that questioned religious government or mentioned sexual activity. In recent times it is directed against any imagery that might make potential readers "uncomfortable," or that might seem contrary to their beliefs. Thus, when *Huckleberry Finn* was first published, people wanted it to be curtailed because it portrayed a friendship between a white boy and a black man. Several decades later it was yanked out of libraries because it portrayed nineteenth-century folks in the south of the USA using the word "nigger." I'd just like to maintain that contrary to what the song claimed, the objects of my affection cannot change my complexion.

Respectfully,
George Bowering

P.S. I am wondering how you feel, comparatively, about Penelope, Molly Bloom, and Honey. Specifically, Penelope's loom, Molly's "Yes," and Honey's "No."

1967 Books

> The list is the mark of a highly advanced, cultivated society because a list allows us to question the essential definitions. The essential definition is primitive compared with the list.
>
> — Umberto Eco

I have been a collector and list maker and archivist all my life. When I am in bed at night, trying to go to sleep, I still do what I did when I was a kid — think of a comic strip character whose name starts with A. Okay, Archie. Now, B. Batman. All right, Cs... The next night it could be cities I have slept in: Anaheim, Boston, Calgary. It could be big league baseball players, five for each letter. Titles of novels. More private items.

In her wonderful essay "Composition as Explanation," Gertrude Stein pretty well told us what we know about lists. One makes a list out of things that are alike (in being names of countries, for example), but you would not have a list unless the items are different from one another. "By lists I mean a series," she said; Jack Spicer would become the foe of manipulative poetics when he began writing what would become known as serial poems. The end of a list is not a climax or a couplet. A series might have the potential to go on forever, unless someone sets a limit, as in the World Series, wherein the first team to collect four wins is this year's champ.

The lists I use to welcome sleep are evanescent, though once in a while I will fill a page of my diary with one. But I also keep lists that record my life as a book person. When I write a poem or a story or an essay, etc., a copy of the MS goes into a binder and gets the date and number recorded on the bottom right side of the last page. When I have about a hundred items in that binder, I make a list of the titles and put it on top and give that binder a name. Then every time I publish one of the poems, say, I write an asterix before its number and name on that title page. I also write the particulars of that publication on the last page of the item. Then I also have some pages at the end of that binder, in which I record details of the publication. Eventually the binders find their way to the National Library (as I still call it), where scholars, if there are any, will have their work made easier for them.

Archivists are familiar with lists. I am not a zealous collector of books, but I do keep certain ones. Once in a while I will get rid of a few thousand books, but there are some I will not part with. In fact I make lists of these keepers. It is an alphabetical list in two sections — Canadian books and other books. I often wish that I lived closer to Powell's Books in Portland; I would buy a lot more books, then. Of course, I have lots of books that don't make it onto these lists. And I don't know how to characterize or name these two lists. I guess you could say that they form the environment for my esthetic, if I have such a fancy thing. Here, I'll give you a hint: Ted Hughes is not on the others list, but Robert Creeley is. I would like to be a completist, but I don't have all of Creeley's books.

There are 97 items on his pages, including books about his work.

Okay, so I list the things I have written and the books I have squirreled away. I have, since I was about thirteen years old, listed the books I have read. I can't tell you when I started to read. My earliest memories of reading involve opening the very wide Vancouver *Province* on the front room floor in Peachland, and figuring out what was happening in the War. I had a white sweatshirt with a bulldog and a Union Jack pictured on it along with the words, "Brittania rules the waves." I must have taken someone's word for that "Brittania." There were a lot of maps in the War news, and one could not help figuring out some of the words on the map and beside it. I thought that after we won the War there would be no more newspapers, and that notion made me sad.

We weren't a bookish family, but it was only natural that books were around, though when you were a child during the Depression and the War you knew that there was no such thing as "disposable income." There were some books at my grandparents' house in Summerland, and I opened them every time we went there. By the time I got old enough to have an allowance, my allowance was five cents a Saturday, and you couldn't get many books for a nickel. But if you could somehow find another nickel you had a comic book, and so when I got to grade three and to a town where there was a drugstore, I started on comic books.

Well, drugstores, eh? They also purveyed magazines and mass-market paperbacks. My life was shaped by drugstores as much as it was by schools. When I had a quarter, I decided, I would buy a movie magazine. For a few months I bought *Modern Screen* and *Photoplay*. Only women movie stars got onto the cover of *Modern Screen*, usually Shirley Temple. If I'd saved my March 1947 issue of *Photoplay* with Bing Crosby on the cover, I'd be able to buy a yacht now.

By 1948, when I was twelve, I had decided that movie mags were not for me, and I got rid of them. I started buying sports magazines, especially baseball magazines. I still have them, except for the hockey mags, which I got rid of a couple of years ago. The first issue of *Sport* that I bought new at the Rexall was for February 1948. It had a rare hockey cover, this one of goalie Frank Brimsek in his Boston Bruins uniform. *Sport* was more interested in horseracing and fly-fishing than they were in the National Hockey League. I suspect that Brimsek made it because unlike most players, he was a USAmerican.

So were most of the authors I bought and read. We had to read some books in school, Robert Louis Stevenson's *Treasure Island* in grade seven, and Robert Louis Stevenson's *Kidnapped* in grade eight. I really liked them. I think that I was the only person in my class, with the possible exceptions of Art Fraser and John Jalovec, to go ahead and read Robert Louis Stevenson's *Black Arrow*. In school, from grade one to grade twelve, it was expected that the girls would get the best marks and the boys would do well to get passed at the end of the year. But I was a secret reader, and I knew that John Jalovec was, too. Art Fraser joked around in class, so I was his ally as well. Jalovec's friend and fellow Slav Joe Makse, joined me in the study hall one period in naming every player in the six-team NHL. Now there was a list.

One day in class John Jalovec said that in the

US the word "Celestial" was used to refer to Chinese immigrants. The teacher said that this was not so. I didn't say anything, but I knew that it was so, because I had read a lot of drugstore westerns in which Chinese cooks and laundrymen showed up. It is not surprising, then, that of the twenty-three books listed on the first page of my reading scribbler, seventeen are westerns. Two are novels by Jack London, two are mysteries by Earle Stanley Gardiner, one is an anthology of crime fiction, and one is the second volume of Ripley's collected "Believe it or Not" items.

Here is what the first line looks like:

CA   1. Blue River Riders   1   Archie Joscelyn

According to a list on the back cover of that first scribbler, CA means Cameo Type, whatever that means. I had something else there, but inked it out and replaced it with CA. I did this, also, with the second book, *Trouble at Moon Pass* by Herbert Shappiro. The third book is *Shot in the Dark*, an anthology edited by Judith Merril for Bantam Books. Just before the title I wrote "B 3". I remember reading it in a big house in the Aiken orchard near Naramata when I was working there. I was thirteen years old. Twenty-five years later I would meet Judith Merril in the Cecil Hotel pub and grill her about the science fiction writers I was reading as a boy. Twenty years after that I would buy a Gertrude Stein first edition that had formerly belonged to John Aiken.

By the way, in those days I was a paperback boy. If I happened to read a clothbound book, the initials before its title would be "GD," which stood for Grosset & Dunlap, a publisher any boy or girl was likely to come across in those days. I used the "GD" designation for the first forty pages of my scribblers. Page 41 began two important changes: I began to write initials for hardback books, and I began to date my entries. Page 41 starts on July 7, 1959, for example, with a book published by Scribners:

SCR   979   Death in the Afternoon   10   Ernest Hemingway

In the early years I used to write in the name of the book as soon as I had well started reading it. I have only about four times in my life not finished reading a book once started. You'll find no listing for *Black Beauty* or *The Bride of Lammermoor*. But before too many years had gone by my puritanism kicked in, and now I do not write in the name of that book until I have finished reading it. At the time of this writing I am thirty pages from writing in the name of Rosemary Sullivan's book about Margaret Atwood.

I have a few other little quirks. At least once every scribbler page I have to repeat an author's name. As soon as I have read ten books by an author I type up the list on half of a sheet of writing paper and staple it to the inside front or back cover of the current scribbler. The most stapled writer is Donald E. Westlake at 100 books. Once in a while I read a page's worth of books by authors whose last names start with the same letter — Sullivan will finish the S page. Sometimes I will run the alphabet down the page — thank goodness for Xenophon. I have read a page's worth of books by women, books by Canadians, books from the nineteenth century, and so on. Once I did a page of authors' first books. As with the alphabet page, I had to make an adjustment to the two-books rule mentioned above.

Well, for some reason my publisher Rolf Maurer found all this interesting, and suggested that we pick a certain year and see what we can make of the books I read that year. I pointed out to him that because of the kind of life I live, I often read a book quite often, Hemingway's *A Farewell to Arms* and H.D.'s *Trilogy*, for examples. I also read an awful lot of magazines and journals and newspapers and student essays and subtitles, and so on. All right, he said, you can mention that. I won't bother, I said.

I said that Mr. Maurer could pick the year. He picked 1967, Canada's centenary, and an important time in our literary history, what with the new small presses and artist-run art galleries and little theatres. It was a kind of momentous year for me, too. I was thirty-one years old. The previous summer I had left my regular job at the University of Calgary, made my first trip to Europe, and snagged a Canada Council grant to start my PhD studies at the University of Western Ontario. In London I met the painter Greg Curnoe, one of my teachers about painting and jazz. So I spent the first half of 1967 in London, Ont. Then along came Sir George Williams University in Montreal and asked me whether I would like to be their writer in residence while Montreal was hosting the World's Fair. I thought it over. On the one hand, Montreal. On the other hand, London. I had been thinking to myself that if I were to get another university job, I'd like it to be at Sir George Williams University or Simon Fraser University, two schools that seemed to be unlike the usual. I decided for Montreal. My wife Angela did not disagree.

While in London I carried on at least three kinds of book-reading. As a doctoral student I was taking several seminars, one on the British Romantics, one on the US nineteenth century, and one on mixed US and Canadian something-or-other, so I was reading for them. I was also reviewing books for a number of magazines and papers, from the Toronto *Globe & Mail* to the Detroit *Fifth Estate*. And then, of course, I was doing my regular leisure reading — William Shakespeare and Jack Kerouac and so on.

So the first Centenary book was:

ML   1611   Prometheus Unbound   3   Percy Bysshe Shelley

I have had a framed poster portrait of Shelley on my writing room wall since 1985, and I have often said that Shelley is the greatest English poet ever. I said it on air from a Vancouver radio station today, as a matter of fact. In the summer of 1963 I heard Allen Ginsberg recite "Mont Blanc" at Jamie Reid's apartment near Coal Harbour in Vancouver, and then a few days later I heard him recite "Adonais" at Stanley Park. Till then I had subscribed to Ezra Pound's attitude toward the Romantic Poets. From then on I shared Allen Ginsberg's. Three years later I was at UWO, learning from Ross Woodman how to read Shelley.

M+S   1612   We Always Take Care of our Own   1   C.J. Newman

Amb	1613	Faces and Forms	3 Anselm Hollo
Scrib	1614	Roots and Branches	4 Robert Duncan
Rye	1615	A Breakfast for Barbarians	3 Gwendolyn MacEwen
EG	1616	Nova Express	4 William S. Burroughs

Maybe I should tell you who some of the publishers were, so that you will get a sense of my system. ML stands for Modern Library. Amb is Ambit, a name that has often been used in publishing, in this case a publisher of non-canonical poetry in London. Scrib is obviously Scribner's, and Rye is Ryerson. Ryerson Press had started as a voice for the United Church of Canada, became a lonely voice for Canadian poetry with the Ryerson Poetry Chapbooks edited by Lorne Pierce and numbering almost two hundred titles from 1925 till 1958, and in the sixties remaining a major player with inventive books by Daphne Marlatt, Lionel Kearns and Dorothy Livesay. Then a US publisher hyphenated Ryerson, dumped poetry, and left us to our own devices. Luckily there arose some dandy devices, such as Coach House Press and Talonbooks. EG, to get back to my list, was the abbreviation for *Evergreen Review*, but stood for Grove Press. This would not be the only time I made things overly complicated.

Auer	1617	The New Handbook Of Heaven	1 Diane di Prima
PQ	1618	Brighton Rock	4 Graham Greene
M+S	1619	Parasites of Heaven	4 Leonard Cohen
Vin	1620	The Temptation Of The West	3 André Malraux
M+S	1621	Let Us Compare Mythologies	5 Leonard Cohen
WR	1622	The Holy Grail	3 Jack Spicer

1967 BOOKS

As you can see, there are a lot of small numbers here, not much in double figures, and in fact a lot of number ones. When I looked at these pages at the outset of this little project I thought the ones might have been caused by my job as a graduate student, but on closer looking I saw that I was reading a lot more outside my courses as I always had at university. As to all those abbreviations you might not know — maybe I should add a list of publishers at the end of this, whatever it is.

DD	1623	From Ritual To Romance 1 Jessie L. Weston
Lan	1624	Lady Sings The Blues 1 Billie Holiday & 1 William Dufty
S	1625	The Legend Of The Wandering Jew 2 Joseph Gaer
Per	1626	Naked Poems 3 Phyllis Webb
Vik	1627	Hart Crane: The Life ... 1 Philip Horton
U.N.	1628	The Deep Truth 1 C.E. Pulos

Every once in a while I somehow find a book that picks me up by the brain and tells me something I needed to know, something that bends the line of learning I have been following, and stands out in my memory and has an effect on the writing, especially the essays, that I do subsequently. One was *Prose Keys to Modern Poetry*, an anthology edited by Karl Shapiro, of essays about writing poetry, most of them by great poets, some by their soul cousins such as Ernest Fenollosa and T.E. Hulme. An earlier one was *The Sullen Art*, David Ossman's interviews with poets such as Robert Creeley, Gilbert Sorrentino and Denise Levertov. Later I plundered Jerome Klinkowitz's *Literary Disruptions*, a book of essays about post-modern

US fiction that does not frame it in European socio-poetic theory. Well, Pulos's *The Deep Truth* was the best book about Shelley's poetry composition that I ever read. It accomplishes the very difficult task of reconciling Shelley's Platonism with his skepticism. And it helps you to get more comfortable with Shelley's proving that the deep truth is imageless.

ND	1629	In the American Grain 15 William Carlos Williams
ML	1630	The House of the Seven Gables 2 Nathaniel Hawthorne
EG	1631	Games People Play 1 Eric Berne, M.D.
ML	1632	The Blithedale Romance 3 Nathaniel Hawthorne
DD	1633	Redburne 2 Herman Melville

It looks as if just about the time our country was turning 100, I was getting into the novels and romances written when the US was around 75. Pretty soon, though, as Montreal loomed in my near future, I could be observed binging on Canadian Literature, celebrated and obscure.

Eliz	1634	To Come To Have Become 3 Theodore Enslin
JC	1635	The Life of John Keats 1 Albert Erlande
OUP	1636	Endymion 1 John Keats
VSH	1637	Letters From The Savage Mind 1 Patrick Lane
S	1638	Pierre, Or The Ambiguities 3 Herman Melville

There are certain novels that become trendy from time to time in English departments and their course outline reading lists. *Pierre, or The Ambiguities* is one of them. Melville produced two, in fact, the other being *The Confidence-Man*. If you are in the Shakespeare crowd, you probably drift toward *Measure for Measure*. I can remember more than once seeing that George Eliot's *Middlemarch* was on half the reading lists for one semester. Conrad people went for *Nostromo* while Faulkner's professors urged *Absalom, Absalom!* I mean back when professors were teaching Faulkner, before Aravind Adiga showed up.

EG	1639	Melville 1 Jean-Jacques Mayoux
B	1640	Billy Budd, Foretopman 4 Herman Melville
Coy	1641	Reading At Berkeley 5 Charles Olson
CBC	1642	The Educated Imagination 1 Northrop Frye

    Well, I figured that if I was going to spend time in the east, where all the bottled food and regular literature came from, I might as well read their big wheel critics and tastemakers. I had spent some time in the west calling this guy North Fried Throwup, and suggesting that some of us back there could get by without seeing the world his way, but I would eventually agree with him about one thing — all writing grows out of previous writing. It's just that the Bible isn't the only source.

    When I got to Sir George Williams University in Montreal, I found out that Margaret Atwood was already there. We managed to take pictures of each other taking pictures of each other in the snow. Perhaps she was thinking of it as an essentially Canadian experience. I thought of it as messing with the idea of taking pictures. *Survival* would come out five years later. It's what House of Anansi was interested in.

EG	1643	Walt Whitman	1 Gay Wilson Allen
RH	1644	Shelley: a Collection of Critical . . .	
		ed. George M. Ridenauer	
Van	1645	The Mechanical Bride	1 Marshall McLuhan

Well, I figured that in case Northrop Frye invaded my psyche, I should take a preventive dose of his University of Toronto colleague. Actually, my old poetry friend Lionel Kearns had been urging McLuhan on me for some time. I thought that maybe that was partly due to the facts that McLuhan was a convert to Catholicism (hence the "Global Village") and that Kearns was an unsuccessfully lapsed Catholic.

Scr	1646	Words	5 Robert Creeley
EG	1647	The Story of O	1 Pauline Réage
RH	1648	Hell's Angels	1 Hunter S. Thompson
M+S	1649	Girls Of Two Summers	1 Gerald Taaffe
RH	1650	When She Was Good	1 Philip Roth
M+S	1651	The Road Past Altamont	1 Gabrielle Roy
M+S	1652	A Jest of God	1 Margaret Laurence

During this time almost all my book reading was done for the reviews I was writing for the *Globe & Mail*. Oh, I was reading a lot of standard "literature" for university, but as you can see, I was reading a lot of authors for the first time. I wondered, as you might, whether a reviewer of famous authors should be new to those authors' work. It turns out that I would become a fan of Philip Roth, so much so that he would become just about my favourite literary writer among those whose books I don't collect. And as for Laurence's book? I eventually wrote the first essay about it, and taught it at several universities, in Canada and abroad, as they say. Even though it has my unlucky number affixed to it here.

M+S 1653 Watcha Gonna Do Boy Watcha . . . 1 Peter Taylor
M+S 1654 Whirlpool 1 Diane Giguère
M+S 1655 Place d'Armes 1 Scott Symons
Ori   1656 Sun Rock Man 1 Cid Corman
M+S 1657 Mirror On The Floor 5 George Bowering

All right, for the first few years I included the books I published. I did read them, eh? But after a while I suffered a crisis of humility and stopped the process. Oh, and while I am here, I should point out that yes, I did capitalize all the words in a title. That is not my practice elsewhere, though. Back to the list, which seems in the early part of 1967 to be McClelland & Stewart's catalogue.

M+S 1658 The Personnel Man 1 Michael Sheldon
M+S 1659 Scratch One Dreamer 1 David Lewis Stein
M+S 1660 Honey In The Rock 1 Christine van der Mark
CB   1661 Zacapa 1 Donn Munson
PQ   1662 The Quiet American 5 Graham Greene
EG   1663 Satori In Paris 17 Jack Kerouac
Rye   1664 The Unquiet Bed 1 Dorothy Livesay

What a history that beautiful slim gold-coloured book had, and in what a number of ways connected with Montreal. I think it was the first book I bought after moving there, from a store on Ste.-Catherine. It was pretty new, and featured art by Roy Kiyooka. Roy was teaching art at Sir George Williams in those days. When I showed him my new purchase, he told me that he had never received a copy from publisher or author. So I gave him mine, hoping, naturally, that I would get one when he got his. Never happened. But decades later I did a reading in Victoria with Al Purdy, and on the drive back to Sidney we decided to stop at Pat Lane's place and wake him up and make him show us where he'd hidden the beer. Pretty soon we were into poet gossip, and pretty soon Dorothy Livesay's name came up. When Pat and I told Al the name of the young male poet from Montreal who was helping to make all that noise with the mature female poet in the unquiet bed, he did a spit-take and claimed not to believe us. I think he did, however, innocent Ontario bard though he was.

M+S	1665	North of Summer 4 Al Purdy
HB	1666	Troilus And Cressida 21 William Shakespeare
CHP	1667	Journeying & The Returns 1 bpNichol
ND	1668	White Mule 16 W. C. Williams
Weed	1669	What They Say 4 John Newlove
Weed	1670	The Poem Poem 1 David McFadden
EG	1671	The Thief's Journal 4 Jean Genet
D	1672	Folk-Rock: The Bob Dylan Story 1 Sy Ribakove & 1 Barbara Ribakove
ND	1673	The Sorrow Dance 5 Denise Levertov
ASB	1674	Charlie Parker 1 Max Harrison
PQ	1675	The Ministry Of Fear 6 Graham Greene

1967 BOOKS

CP	1676	The Debauched Hospodar 1 Guillaume Apollinaire
EG	1677	The War In Algeria 1 Jules Toy
CP	1678	Total War 2 Harry Howith

I still have that Howith book. It's in mint condition except for my name written on the inside. I just saw it listed for $200 on the web. You never can tell.

| OP | 1679 | The Ginger Man 1 J.P. Donleavy |
| DP | 1680 | The Hypocritic Days 3 Douglas Woolf |

Anyone who knows what was going on in the new American fiction in the sixties knows how important Douglas Woolf's first book was, and how hard it was, even in the sixties, to find a copy. It was published by young Robert Creeley in his Majorca-based Divers Press, a hand-sewn little item that for me was just the opposite of the Graham Greene books I was eating up in those days. Graham Greene was a good writer and for me a guilty pleasure, as they say. I liked his writing though he was not "one of us," just as later would be the case with Philip Roth and Toni Morrison.

OS	1681	The Fork 1 Richard Duerden
Bkly	1682	Go Up For Glory 2 Bill Russell & 1 William McSweeney
GP	1683	The Last Of The Crazy People 1 Timothy Findley
Rye	1684	Pointing 3 Lionel Kearns
Bra	1685	School For Wives 3 Alexander Trocchi
Bra	1686	White Thighs 4 Alexander Trocchi

HAP   1687   Kingdom Of Absence 1 Dennis Lee
PQ   1688   The Confidential Agent 7 Graham Greene
VSH   1689   From The Portals Of Mouseholes 1 Seymour Mayne

    Reading Seymour Mayne had something to do with coming from Vancouver to live in Montreal. He had recently gone from Montreal to Vancouver, to take Creative Writing, I think. Just after our mimeographed and then offset *Tish* started publishing in the early fall of 1961, there came to us a mimeo mag from Montreal called *Cataract*. Its main editor seemed to be Mayne, and its gaggle of poets included K.V. Hertz, Avi Boxer and Henry Moscovitch, followers, they believed, of Irving Layton. They proclaimed their belligerency, and opposed the Tish poets' interest in poetics. They proclaimed that the poetic process involved seeing some thigh or blood and getting explosive about it. *Cataract* lasted for less than two years, and the exhortatory poets seemed to scatter to other provinces or into silent apartments.

    I lived in Montreal for four years, and the poetry scene was pretty varied. There were lots of French-language poets, the most interesting being those connected with the very good journal *La Barre du jour*. There were the greyheads who had long defined Quebec poetry in English for the Toronto critics — F.R. Scott, A.J.M. Smith, Ralph Gustafson and John Glassco (who would become our bootlegger during the liquor strikes). You will notice that there aren't any female names here, though I always took Nicole Brossard to be the most interesting of the Francophone writers. Leonard Cohen was in the US by then, and D.G. Jones didn't get into town all that often.

1967 BOOKS

A third batch would be made up of the conservative and academic poets who would later take over the Véhicule Press and save it from its avant-garde ways.

The fourth group was made up mainly by very young poets, Artie Gold and Endre Farkas and others, well documented by their member Ken Norris. And there was the peripatetic Roy Kiyooka.

EG	1690	Baal Babylon 2 Fernando Arrabal
ND	1691	The Owl 3 John Hawkes
ND	1692	The Goose On The Grave 4 John Hawkes

All right, that was kind of cheating. What I read was a book that included those two Hawkes novellas. I apologize now. It was about this time that Hawkes was becoming my favourite living author — no, writer. He was so beautifully difficult. In later years he would leave New Directions for a bigger-deal publisher, and his stories would get more psychological and easier to read. I heard him read only once, at McGill, so there was another good thing about that time in Montreal.

D	1693	Black Is Best 1 Jack Olsen
Cit	1694	My Art, My Life 1 Diego Rivera & 1 Gladys March
PQ	1695	Our Man In Havana 8 Graham Greene
M+S	1696	Periods Of The Moon 12 Irving Layton
EG	1697	The Soft Machine 5 William S. Burroughs
EG	1698	The Beard 5 Michael McClure
ND	1699	By The Waters Of Manhattan 1 Charles Reznikoff
CHP	1700	Nevertheless, These Eyes 1 Roy Kiyooka
S	1701	How To Be A Jewish Mother 1 Dan Greenberg

Hey, I was planning to live in Montreal for a while.

CJ	1702	Signs Of A Migrant Worrier 4 Douglas Woolf
Oyez	1703	The Years As Catches 5 Robert Duncan
CHP	1704	One / Eye / Love 1 Victor Coleman
Noon	1705	Listen, Little Man 1 Wilhelm Reich
ECE	1706	Water I Slip Into At Night 3 Margaret Randall
CI	1707	Bread, Wine And Salt 2 Alden Nowlan
CHP	1708	Baseball 6 George Bowering
PQ	1709	The Lost Childhood 9 Graham Greene
HAP	1710	The Circle Game 1 Margaret Atwood

I have now read 40 books by Margaret Atwood, and have number 41 lined up. I had the Contact Press edition of *The Circle Game* (1964) and would often read poems in it, but I guess that it was not until Peggy gave me a pre-publication copy of the House of Anansi edition that I sat right down and read it through. I thought that the Contact edition was nicer to look at and hold, but Contact was not known for keeping its backlist in print.

4S	1711	Love Lion Book 6 Michael McClure
M+S	1712	The Spice-Box Of Earth 6 Leonard Cohen
HB	1713	Mrs. Dalloway 1 Virginia Woolf
M-H	1714	Ezra Pound: A Close-Up 1 Michael Reck
PL	1715	Son Of A Smaller Hero 3 Mordecai Richler
PQ	1716	Stamboul Train 10 Graham Greene

* * *

The publishers and their abbreviations. In my first pages there was not much of a problem. Most of the books I was reading were mass-market paperbacks available at the Rexall or the Friendly Corner across from the New Oliver Theatre. B stood for Bantam Books, P for Pocket Books, D for Dell, S for Signet (the New American Library). A stood for Avon Books, GM for Gold Medal (Fawcett), PL for Popular Library, H for Harlequin (yes, in the early days they published other genres), WC for Collins White Circle (I think they came, like Harlequins, from Winnipeg). PA was Pan, AO was Ace Originals, and for some reason I cannot remember but which I still respect, Penguin Books was responsible for PQ. You might not be surprised that for a while I kept track of the number of books by each publisher.

If you are a reader who finds lists at all interesting, you are likely here. If you would like to skip the next paragraph, it's all right. There should be a limit to some things. I don't think that I would be able to tell you what all the initials of 1967 stand for, but I can offer a few tries.

EG stands for Grove Press, and was taken from the name of Grove's literary magazine *Evergreen Review*. Auer is short for Auerhahn Press, which was founded by printer Dave Haselwood, who printed the first books of a lot of San Francisco poets. M+S means McClelland & Stewart, who billed themselves as "The Canadian Publishers." Vin stands for Vintage, one of the leaders in "quality paperbacks" of the time. WR is White Rabbit, a San Francisco poets' press started by Joe Dunn to publish Robert Duncan, Jack Spicer, and their circle. DD is Doubleday, just like the crest sewn on the baseball jackets of the Auburn Doubledays of the New York-Penn League. Per is short for Periwinkle Press, the short-lived outfit run by painter Tak Tanabe and Robert Reid, who made nice books at Klanak Press. Periwinkle would publish beautifully designed books by John Newlove, Gerry Gilbert and Roy Kiyooka, as well as Phyllis Webb's remarkable *Naked Poems*. They were going to do a book of my stories but the ephemerality of time swept us apart. Vik stands for Viking, of course, and ND stands for New Directions, the most important US publisher when it comes to modernist poetry. ML is Modern Library. Eliz is short for *Elizabeth*, a small poetry magazine and press in New Rochelle, N.Y. OUP is the familiar Oxford University Press. Less familiar is VSH, which stands for Very Stone House, a mimeograph press run by the aforementioned Seymour Mayne and Pat Lane on the west coast. Coy is short for *Coyote's Journal*, an Oregon magazine that occasionally had the nerve to emit something like a book. CBC stands, of course, for the CBC. RH is Random House. Vang and Van both stand for Vanguard. Scr is Scribner's. Orig is short for *Origin*, Cid Corman's key poetry journal and the few books it managed. Rye is the ironic abbreviation for the Ryerson Press, which was run by the Canadian United Church. Brand and Bran are Brandon House, a little paperback outfit where Scottish novelist Alexander Trocchi published his pornographic fiction. HAP means House of Anansi Press. CHP is Coach House Press. CJ is another way of abbreviating *Coyote's Journal*. Oyez is the actual name printed on broadsides and books printed by David Haselwood and later Graham Mackintosh, with a concentration on Bay Area poets. Noon was short for Noonday Press. ECE means the books published by the Mexican literary magazine *El corno emplumado*. CI means Clarke, Irwin. 4S indicated Four Seasons, another San Francisco poetry press.

1967 BOOKS

A keen eye will note that I didn't catch them all here. But there is an old saying in the archives world: "Aaagh, close enough!"

My editors have both told me that it would be kind of interesting to know how many of these books I still have in "their actually-read editions," as one of them phrased it so elegantly. Well, quite a few, though there would be a lot more if some events of the first year in this century had not occurred. That's when I sold my enormous Kerrisdale house and moved to a little 2400 square feet house in West Point Grey. Losing the majority of my shelf-space meant selling and otherwise abandoning most of my books, getting the thousands down to the few thousands. So while I kept all my Gertrude Stein books and Robert Kelly books, I said goodbye to all my Henry James books and Fyodor Dostoyevsky books. It was easy to do but not easy to let happen. As it was, I had to get Paul Naylor to build bookshelves in almost every room in our new house. But now if I want to read a Graham Greene book again I have to head to a used-book store.

So. Of the 106 books I read during our centenary, I still have 54.

Oh, and yesterday I bought another copy of *On the Road*. There's no room on the *On the Road* shelf.

> We make lists because we don't want to die.
> — Umberto Eco

Apollinaire and Vancouver: A Story about Our Poetry

When I was a boy living in a semi-arid Podunk called Oliver, British Columbia, I used to imagine other places. Sometimes a young person would have help doing this. My boyhood came before television, thank God. With television you don't use your imagination. With radio you did, back in the day when radio had dramas instead of whatever it has now. With books, too, you did. The hundreds of westerns I read as a boy called for my imagination, even though the landscapes their authors described were pretty much what I saw in the cactussy south Okanagan valley every day.

But when I would read a USAmerican novel about winning World War II in Europe or Asia, my mind was in a landscape or seascape I had never been surrounded by. I had to invent a little, maybe calling on photographs from *Life* magazine. When I got around to reading *Catcher in the Rye*, I found it a little hard to put myself in the place of the rich kid narrator who knew his way around New York City and had the money to ride in taxicabs. I had to rely on other stories set in New York, and photographs in *Life* magazine.

A year earlier I had read *Nineteen Eighty-four*, and kind of enjoyed imagining a world seen from a sort of British point of view thirty-five long years in the future. (Those years looked a lot shorter from the other end, of course.) But then my grade eleven English teacher gave me hell for doing my book report on some science fiction in a pocket book.

"Actually," I said, "it's a Signet Book, otherwise called the New American Library." I was, by then, begun on my commitment to archive my reading life.

"You know what I mean," said my grade eleven English teacher.

This was the same person whose subject in composition class was always either the wrong way to form an English sentence, or what was "understood" rather than said.

I decided that I would write poetry. It didn't matter where you were in poetry — unless you were Robert Frost or one of his guys. My first long poem was about headhunters in Malacca. Till today I have no idea whether there ever were such people — in the original sense. Luckily, I lent my only copy of the poem to a friend's girlfriend, and as such things transpire, I never got it back. So much for the imagination, or as Percy Shelley would have had it, the fancy.

Anyway — when I was a book-reading boy in desert-like Oliver, BC, I often heard of a municipality called Hope, BC, perhaps because my uncle Jack and some other people were building the Hope-Princeton Highway. Geographically and historically, Hope is very important to British Columbia, so somehow in my juvenile imagination, or let's say fancy, Hope became a city, with at least modest skyscrapers and canyon-like city streets. Now picture the impact of realism when our highschool brass band went to New Westminster for that city's famous Easter celebration — and on the way there the train eased out of the Coquihalla Valley and stopped for a few minutes in Hope, BC.

Okay, I thought, but there will be skyscrapers and so

on in Vancouver and New Westminster. Around that time the population of Vancouver was about a quarter of what it is sixty-five years later, and people back then lived closer to the ground. It's true — for some reason people living in newish cities in western Canada liked to brag about their few tallish buildings. In Vancouver the World Tower, an aggressively named Beaux-Arts edifice named for the mayor's newspaper that would occupy it for a short time, was built in 1911–12. It was seventeen storeys high, plus a three-storey dome. It was, Vancouverites would always remind you, "The Tallest Building in the British Empire." But in 1930 the Art Deco Marine Building would open, claiming for a while that boastful title seized from its rival a few city blocks to the east.

Of course, if you dropped these two buildings vertically into the river district of Chicago, they would pretty well disappear. But in addition to a handful of junior skyscrapers, the city on Canada's west coast had a couple of romances going — and Chicago, remember, was basically hog-butcher for the world, if you believed USAmerican poetry. If you believed French poetry, though, Vancouver had the romance of the fur trade and the romance of the transcontinental railroad. Both of these romances took place in darkness and snow.

The great Guglielmo Alberto Wladimiro Alessandro Apollinaire de Kostrowitzky, a Polish Italian who composed modernist French poetry under the name of Guillaume Apollinaire, wrote:

> Étincelant diamant
> Vancouver
> Où le train blanc de neige et de feux nocturnes fuit l'hiver...

Apollinaire wrote quite a few poems with Canadian references, and he is usually called a Cubist or Surrealist poet — make of that what you will.

But the fifth line of the poem in question, "Windows," says, when translated into English, "We will send it by telephone." The story goes that Apollinaire was sitting in a street café with some friends, when he suddenly remembered that he was supposed to be writing an introduction to a show by his painter friend Robert Delaunay. The show was called "*Les fenêtres.*" Lots of critics think that the first line of the poem by Apollinaire and his drinking buddies was a reference to Delaunay's art: "*Du rouge au vert tout le jaune se meurt.*" I think that like the fifth line, it tells us where the collaborators were, near a Paris traffic light, a device almost as modern as the telephone. (You will recall that Hugh Kenner, in denying that Yeats was a modernist, asked whether we can imagine a telephone in a Yeats poem.) That first line directs our poem's traffic: "From red to green all the amber dies." Well, the first traffic light appeared in Montmartre a year before the poem, but it was not red, green and amber. Either Apollinaire bent time to his wishes, or revisited the poem in the future.

Are we still talking about Vancouver and the poetic imagination? As I have said, Apollinaire sprinkled his poems with references to Canada. Our country returned the favour: in the Quebec town of Sainte-Apollinaire, there is the factory of a company named Laflamme that sells the EcoNova window. Sounds to me like an early twentieth-century art and literature movement.

All right. If you were going to write a critical piece about "*Les fenêtres,*" you might note that, perhaps because it was collaborative, the poem scatters about for most of its length, then is brought together about the time that the single-word line "Vancouver" appears. That proceeds to an ending with a window that opens like an orange (or a painting) that is both fruit and colour, both of those the opposite to the winter that Vancouver train is fleeing.

If you have a look at Delaunay's windows you will see the simultaneity and colours that make the poem a nice exhibition note for the paintings. Delaunay's windows are made of colour, not to be seen through like any nineteenth-century French painter's window on nature, but to be seen. It is in Delaunay that we can see as we have seen elsewhere, that modern painting showed modern writing the way. Something the Vancouver poets would learn half a century later.

Apollinaire's Swiss friend, Frédéric Louis Sauser, lost his right arm in World War I, and became the great left-handed French poet Blaise Cendrars. He would be an inveterate traveller and writer of poems composed or set in foreign parts. His friend Apollinaire received shrapnel wounds to the head during that same war and died from the great flu epidemic two days before the Armistice, hence never travelling to the Vancouver of his poem.

It is not likely that Cendrars travelled to the Vancouver of his poem, either. The poet who claimed to have been born in Paris lived a fictive life. Though coming from a bourgeois Swiss family, he would present himself as an ultra-whitmanic roustabout with a cheap suitcase checking out scalping knives in a "squaw's wigwam," or "looking for a cheap hotel" in Vancouver's dark side.

Cendrars would go to Hollywood twenty-five years after writing "Far West," a longish fauvist poem. There he wrote articles on Tinseltown and sent them to the newspaper *Paris-Soir*. His writing about the city he did see and his writing about exotic places he never got to are quite similar. A lot of it is made up, as was the personage he presented in place of himself. Having lost his right arm, he would indulge a taste for the darkly romantic, say the sinister. Even his Vancouver of 1912, though, begins with the gothic's favourite weather — fog:

> You can hardly hear the bell of ten p.m. through
> the thick fog that blankets piers and boats,

and we are tipped off that what follows will be mysterious and hostile to human sense. The wind will be glacial and the shadows murky. Steamships are gone to mysterious Asia and to a "Klondike" that the poet must have thought was on some Pacific coast. When the first person arrives he resembles a noir private eye:

> In the gloom I strain to make out street signs
>   while I haul my valise,
>   looking for a cheap hotel.

Early in the twentieth century in Europe the artists and poets looked for history's alternative within the human psyche, deranging the senses and swimming through dreams. In places such as Vancouver, as far from Europe as they could get or fancy getting, they saw that history was being held away by a dark scary exotic. People on the northwest coast didn't live in history as they did even in Quebec City, but in myth. The surrealists, especially André Breton, collected aboriginal art from the coast around and north of Vancouver, feeling a companionship and a source provided by imagination that never had to free itself from Aristotle and the French Academy.

Not long after the middle of the century, a San Francisco poet with a taste for surrealism and baseball would write a serial poem called *Seven Poems for the Vancouver Festival*. Jack Spicer wrote this "Magazine Verse" in the spring of 1965, a last composition before his death a few months later. He was planning on a move to Vancouver, where several of his San Francisco associates had already relocated, but he knew that he might be heading for a different location. Robin Blaser wrote that Vancouver had given Spicer "a brief sense of beginning again" (not a bad description of the experience of making a serial poem), but he went down to the Bay Area for the 1965 poetry jamboree, and died there before the summer was gone.

So his last poem would not work its way through everyday life and its objects, say on a Vancouver pier, but head for the surrounding hills:

> Start with a baseball diamond high
> In the Runcible Mountain wilderness.

And if I were a poet instead of a reader here, I would be permitted to say that Spicer's diamond high above the city

> *Étincelant diamant*
> *Vancouver*

These poets are not playing around — they are dying.

Jack Spicer's subjects were baseball and poetry, and neither was a diversion, neither was just entertainment. Diamonds are not temporary.

People who live in myth do not understand the use of entertainment. Put it another way: Apollinaire, Cendrars and Spicer were not describing or recording Vancouver — they were spinning it. And Runcible Mountain? You likely know that "runcible" is a nonsense adjective invented by Edward Lear. The Owl and the Pussycat, remember, shared a "runcible spoon." You may be less likely to know that Jack Spicer was a friend of the science fiction author Philip K. Dick, and that their works shared ideas and themes, that Dick's fictions were frequented by a character named Leo Runcible.

So you see, Vancouver has not all that often been a setting for poetic realists. To be fair, I will say that while Malcolm Lowry was squatting in and near the city, he toiled on prose about hallucinatory Mexico, but he also wrote doggedly iambic sonnets about skid road Vancouver. French poets might find diamonds among the rough, but twentieth-century Brits (and would-be Brits) tended to curl a lip and notice dirty feet. In a typical poem titled "Christ Walks In This Infernal District Too," Lowry is not looking for any snow-covered locomotive, but rather for drug addicts stumbling into despicable beer parlours. Do you want to know the relationship between nature and the human? Windows don't open like oranges for Lowry, but "chancres blossom like the rose,"

> For on each face is such a hard despair
> That nothing like a grief could enter there.
> And on this scene from all excuse exempt

The mountains gaze in absolute contempt

There's another Englishman, we said, making the internal external.

The realists thought or said that they were recording a world — or a city — instead of spinning one. But you will recall that Lowry's unfortunate consul was told, as a jailed Lowry was told in Oaxaca, "you say you a wrider but we read all your wridings and dey don't make sense. You no wrider, you an espider and we shoota de espiders in mejico." (p. 29 in the Signet edition). We know that Lowry's protagonist had a head that was spinning much of the time, but when it came to poetry it was time for sober reflection.

Lowry spent the time of World War II in Vancouver and the North Shore, unwillingly for the most part, if you believe his letters. He did not romanticize the aboriginal world, but rather displayed the normal British racism in his remarks about non-Europeans. He really wanted to get back to California, but the US would not let him back in. He said that he would enlist in England if England would pay his travel expenses. He saw Canadians enlisting in droves, and while he did refer to Vancouver as "an outpost of Empire" when he wasn't calling it "The Slough of Despond," he did not seem to entertain the idea of wearing a Canadian uniform, no matter how much it resembled the British one. Nor did he look for a non-combatant's job. He had come from a non-working background, and for people such as he, the word "income" meant what the family settled on one. In a famous fall 1939 letter to Conrad Aiken, its pages filled with self-pity, he says that he and his girlfriend Marjorie stay in bed beneath one thin cover because it is "the only place in Vancouver where we have found either pleasure or protection." Vancouver he called "the most hopeless of all cities of the lost," where the dramatic mock-tragic couple huddles in bed "like gaboons in the jungle to keep warm, no blankets or one, and pinchbeck overcoats: we freeze: the icy rain which hasn't stopped for days doesn't even bring melancholy any longer: the room is damp, muscles contract with rheumatiz, noses run, we cough like sheep, I fear Margie may become really ill. We haven't had enough to eat, one plate of beans a day," etc. This in a city where quite a few people wear shorts in November. And things weren't all that much better in Warsaw that fall.

Well, if you read Lowry's most inventive novel *October Ferry to Gabriola*, you will encounter a couple that runs into very bad weather everywhere they go in Canada. Lowry and his fictional protagonists are lightning rods of the pathetic fallacy.

Remember the small-town boy George Bowering, who never got to see novels and stories and poems that took place in his locale? He grew up and moved to Vancouver, and started writing novels and stories and poems about his boyhood south Okanagan and his adulthood Vancouver. He looked for literature about this new place. He read John Dos Passos's *The 42nd Parallel*, in which some itinerant guys take the train from Manitoba to the west coast. He noted that Thomas Wolfe got sick on a ferry from the Island to Vancouver and died of meningitis right after getting back to Baltimore. Bowering's beloved Aunt Dorothy died of the same disease that same month.

He read Earle Birney, who was a pretty good friend of Malcolm Lowry's widow. Birney published two novels, but one was set in England and the other in Utah. He did write poems and radio stuff about Vancouver and its environs, stuff mainly geological and historical and what we would later call ecological.

Late in his life the kid would read the literary record left by Pauline Johnson, Emily Carr and Irene Baird, appreciating their mythological understanding of the place.

Ah, place! How often I hear or read a poet say that he or she is driven by a sense of place. You know that I was that kid who wanted to experience the thrill of reading poetry and fiction (and opera in the case of Barbara Pentland) made by and about the place that literally made me. So I would rush to read the work of the writer who mentioned his or her attention to place. I would wind up reading something like a poem titled "Vancouver," that wears these lines:

> sailboats dotting the bay,
> picknickers at crowded beaches
> competing for summer heat
> and precious square centimetres of sand.

The writer was a political scientist rather than a poet, but he did publish that poem among others of similar cast.

To see what I am complaining about, you have only to do something like this:

> Hondas jamming the pay lot,
> shoppers in crowded boutiques
> fighting over winter jackets
> and precious made in China frocks.

I'm pretty sure that you could all play this game. But that is not enough to make art. Shelley did not describe Mont Blanc. Coleridge did not list the dangers of a sea voyage. H.D. did not look around for some recommended metaphors to tell us what London was like during the blitz.

Sure, sometimes I like to take a rest and read poems by the find-your-own-voice, write-what-you-know crowd. These people, if they are liked by the reviewers, are said to be masters, in control of their art. In another profession they might be in control of the acreage they are getting down in words, turning a forest into Forest Heights Estates, for example. Instead of committing "development," they settle for describing nature and other environments. In order to do this, they often like to make similies. If someone wants to know what a place is like, it's because he wants to be able to settle it among his previous experiences. Write what you know, indeed. Know what you write. Don't be a stranger.

"The power is there," said Shelley. "Nah, it's right here," said the developer poet. You might tell me that you have found similies in "Mont Blanc." Listen again, I say. "And what were thou, and earth, and stars, and sea, / If to the human mind's imaginings / Silence and solitude were vacancy?"

At times during my life I have heard people who are supposed to know more than I do extolling someone's efforts to "conquer nature." That phrase has always made me flinch. I learned to associate it with finding your own voice and writing what you know and being in control of your material. Milton Acorn, a sometime Vancouver poet who was a lot better than his admirers, often sold himself short because he liked a fight, and once said in a good interview, "A poet should write about what he or she knows." Take that, Apollinaire and Cendrars. Take that, Shelley.

Now, the funny thing about Shelley was that while he saw secrets and mysteries as the animators of his subject, he read everything that scholars and scientists wrote, and all the encyclopaediae he could obtain. He knew the scientific theories about atoms and volcanoes, and leaned on them in ordering his revolutionary poems. If some Oxford professors suggested writing about what he knew, Shelley had already left the building.

Now I will turn to a poet who never had anything good to say about Percy Shelley, but who had flirted a little with Keats. In one lecture, Charles Olson would say that the scholar poet should study his subject — whales, Idaho, trilobites — until he knows more about it than anyone else in the room; in another lecture he would stand with Keats, who championed negative capability, being inside doubts, mystery, etc. Shelley said that that's what, rarely as it occurred, was the "spirit of delight." That's when a lot of poets say "get me out of here." But place, if it is to be anything but backdrop, is not something to be entered and exited, not something to dot with sailboats or describe with comparisons. It has a way, does place, of getting inside your soul.

Now I am going to try to say something I've been trying to settle into for as long as I can remember. Since first reading it, I have loved William Carlos Williams's long, long poem *Paterson*, named after a city I have never visited. It is a poem utterly unlike, say, Carl Sandburg's "Chicago," or William Wordsworth's "London 1802," and not just because it is long. Williams proposes in his author's note "that a man in himself is a city, beginning, seeking, achieving and concluding his life in ways which the various aspects of a city may embody." This he published in the first edition of the first book of the poem. Things changed as the poem proceeded. But what we learned for sure is that *Paterson* would not be a setting against which poetic stuff would happen.

A critic named Peterson tried to make it simple for us WCW acolytes: "the city's relation to its landscape is emblematic of man's relation to his world, and it is primarily the latter which *Paterson* is 'about'." I will leave it to you to see whether Williams's omnitrope sinks into your own human sense of things. For sure, though, no reader is going to be able to follow this as just another Google Earth poem.

Spoiler alert. I was one young poet in a group of young poets who had William Carlos Williams as a grandfather. Our father was a guy named Charles Olson, a poet not well known to the English departments in, say, 1960. We read and quoted his essays and poems all hours of the day and night, especially the essay "Projective Verse." Eventually some patriotic poets back east would accuse us of slavishly following some US poetry bosses, but Olson's strongest advice was that we should attend to the circumstances we found ourselves in. Pretty soon the little poetry newsletter we produced each month would have maps of Greater Vancouver on the covers, and we would be repeating one of Olson's favourite words — locus. The word is Greek for place, of course, but we knew enough to nose around among its usages.

In all of them, in history, genetics, mathematics,

biology, locus is not just another name for place. It is a site where something important is happening. When the human universe (a term from Shelley that Olson didn't seem to mind using) is considered, that place is where your being — or mine — is a verb. In his Einsteinish *The Special View of History*, Olson makes the case for defining history from the inside out. Communist thinkers among others talk about history as a force that picks us up and moves us. Olson's history is a word for what we all do, we humans being: "man is no trope of himself as a synecdoche of his species, but is, as actual determinant, each one of us, a conceivable creator." An actor, not an acted upon.

And as in time, so in space. We are not figures in a landscape. The landscape does not exist without us. In the Lowry poem I quoted, the human beings are acted upon, and they are looked on by nature as a "scene." When Shelley, on the other hand, told us of the secret caverns at the apex of Mont Blanc, that the power was "there," he did so in a poem that begins with the Humean view that "The everlasting universe of things / Flows through the mind."

And how does the human, while he is being, perceive his place in the world and time? Here we come to another word we tyros snatched from Olson — proprioception. Stripping the printed version of Olson's lecture on the subject of upper case letters, we get "sensibility within the organism by movement of its own tissues." A little later, down the page and over in the margin, "the soul is / proprioceptive."

All right. The poet and Vancouver. You will often come across phrases such as "the life of the poet," or "the poet's life." You will find such life, if the poet is any good, in his poems. In his body his tissues are moving, and his body perceives that motion, and in his action he is history, he is locus, he is temporary, and if he is a careful listener, we can feel his experience in all our own senses.

I would like to tell you about a few of my favourite poems written by Vancouverites who read Olson when they were young. I think that the sharpest portrayal of the relationship between proprioception and locus comes in Daphne Marlatt's oft-published booklength poem *Steveston*. The settlement at the mouth of the Fraser River was important to the Japanese and Canadian salmon-fishing worlds. In the poem we are shown women, usually, who have to work on a floor that moves as the river's flow and the ocean's tide move; see the woman cooking cabbage rolls, who "walks, from counter to stove, with a roll." That's not a pun; that's a rime, one of many that imitate, too, the watery world. The poet abides in the world of her poem, I venture to say, in like manner, poetic feet at the ends of sea legs.

Sorry.

Marlatt's first long poem of note was *Vancouver Poems*, one volume in a set of four booklength poems written by Tish poets and published by Coach House Press in 1972. It would, in ways too numerous to detail, differ from Earle Birney's famous longish poem about moving feet and mind through our city's centre.

"November Walk Near False Creek Mouth" (1961) is a poem of its time, or perhaps of its author's time. Birney was Canada's most prominent poet in the period covering Depression and Cold War, and he was also a teacher of old and middle English verse, so it is not surprising to hear satire and Chaucerian scansion in his walking poem. He does not so much take his scene in, nor give over to its demands, as he characterizes it with orderly rhythm and alliteration and bravura metaphor:

> The tree-barbed tip of Point Grey's lance
> has failed again to impale the gone sun
> Clouds and islands float together
> out from the darkening bandsaw of suburbs
> and burn like sodium over the distant waters

Oddly, we remember that Birney had years earlier written a radio play titled *Trial of a City*, because throughout this walking poem we are aware that the city is being judged, that the poem is a kind of trail of evidence, and that it hints at a punishment in the form of nuclear Armageddon, a theme that appears elsewhere in Birney's work:

> a young girl sits on a granite bench
> so still as if already only
> silhouette burned in the stone

It is November, after all. The end portends.

Once in a while the judge becomes not quite the archaeologist that Olson likes to see in his own work, but at least an observer:

> and I on the path at the high-tide edge
> wandering under the leafless maples
> between the lost salt home
> and the asphalt lodge where carhorns call
> call in the clotting air by a shore
> where shamans never again will sound

[are you hearing all this lovely rime?]

> with moon-snail conch the ritual plea
> to brother salmon or vanished seal
> and none ever heard
> the horn of Triton or merman

[oops, classical allusions edge the aboriginal inhabitants away.]

In reading the poem you are aware mostly of the rhythm, but images come through and stick. Sometimes, though, you wonder about an old boat resting on "an Ararat of broken clamshells." It's clever, but it isn't Vancouver. Still, this is a memorable poem, and we snobs in time forgive it.

Daphne Marlatt's *Vancouver Poems* was written a decade later, and while it is in most ways very much different from Birney's flânerie, it shares a devotion to highly noticeable sound, and when the expanded version of Marlatt's poem was published in 2013, it was retitled *Liquidities*, a word used in Birney's poem.

I am pretty sure that I am not the only contemporary who wondered about that plural in the original title. The work is clearly a sequence, perhaps a serial poem, and it even suggests a kind of flânuese's walk from beginning to end. Reading from the first to the last unnumbered page, you find yourself going from residential neighbourhood down to the waterfront and from this present to an earlier time of pioneer loggers, then to aboriginal coast, and finally to this mysterious and near perfect ending:

                              under
carboniferous imprint of old fern, echinoidea, solaster,
we step back in space before the drift & diamond light
fail — to see you, call

                    Worm, small worm host of light.
Borrow a shell.

Yes, you saw or heard the diamond is back. But did you see "no idea" in echinoidea?

Birney and Marlatt, beings moving in their ways through the city. A Daphne Marlatt poem is noticeably a graph (or trail) of a human's senses in motion, proprioception, I guess, in place. I would like to borrow my daughter Thea's way of watching a Marlatt poem: "a radical poetic such as Baudelaire's begins with the writer in the present, lost in language, writing without intent, and yet in a state of extreme concentration." You'll have no problem in seeing the difference between Birney's walk and Marlatt's.

You will see in the first page of Marlatt's poem that you have to let yourself be lost in (not thought but) language, intently concentrating the while. Take the third word of the poem, "wavers". The line is "Wet fur wavers". That word could be a verb, or it could be a noun. And that choice bifurcates the whole book to come, and there are more bifurcations to come.

Now alerted, the attentive reader will hear/see the word "Asphalt" and expect "as fault" to cut "thru time," as the repeated "salt" does. You will need light feet to show you the ways through this lovely poem. (Oh, and Birney uses "asphalt" in his poem, but not this way.)

You want to know how proprioception will get you through or around? Imagine a young blind poet with the ambition to find his own syllabic way as a walker of a city, say Vancouver. This is Ryan Knighton. He was born in the very early seventies, diagnosed with retinitis pigmentosa as a teen, wrote poems while his eyesight disappeared, made witticisms about Milton, wrote two successful autobiographical books, and turned his attention to writing for motion pictures. Not many blind people do that.

In 2001 he published his first full book of poetry, a third of which is the sequence "From Charles Street, Pandemonium." You get the Milton reference, right? In fact, the young poet has the nerve to introduce the epic poet right off the bat: "In Milton's plot, his paradise / inside a darkness / is unearthed by God." The old blind poet will be the young poet's companion, usually called "John," in some wandering in the young poet's home environment in the east end and elsewhere in Vancouver.

Thus we see the young poet's prepared structure, and recognize that his work will resemble Birney's in some ways, while edging toward the discovered form of Marlatt's. The world of psychology gives us the term "ego dissolution" to name what happens in Marlatt's poem, where the boundary between self and surround loses definition. "I is the other," averred Baudelaire's successor Arthur Rimbaud. Everyone knows this. On seeing man's first home, Milton's Satan complains, "Which way I fly is Hell; myself am Hell." It's all in your mind, said Shelley's hero David Hume.

In Pandemonium, totally deprived of Heaven's light, how did demons and author see? Why, with "darkness visible." Ryan Knighton's poem is chased with images created by Robert Sherrin, photographs obviously of things, but unfocused. The poem evokes memories of Vancouver seen, but of neighbourhoods disappearing from sight, haunted by Miltonic paradoxes. Knighton may just be writing of Milton when he says:

> The vision is that
> purifying, that searing
> it blackened his eyes

but then:

> It is not a hard world
> to justify, to be touched into
> by blindness. I imagine the words

and the sentence goes on, but the notation stops it nicely there for a tap of a cane's time.

So the poem is the walk of a poet going blind in the heart of his city. In offering an ordinary guy by calling his epic companion simply John, the young new poet faces us with a necessary trust. Someone says casually near the end of the poem, "It is not / a great poem," and we say this is no city for masterpieces. Maybe ego dissolution has been entering with the darkness. Knighton says goodbye to his Virgil-like walking friend John, and says in a Vancouverite's demotic:

> us would-be flaneurs wait for
> oblivion in its pleasing shape
> of love, our common
>
> emergency.

This is said in the final section of the poem, thirteen little stanzas that treat of the speaker's understanding of his task, to render the unseen seen:

> But how
> do you go on
> to make this place
>
> out of this place?
>
> . . . .
>
> What I saw
> & couldn't was that grace-
> ful body
>
> . . . .
>
> as beauty seems
>
> sometimes best
> seems served
>   blindly.

Ryan Knighton was one of the Tads in a poets' group called Dads and Tads in the nineties. These people took turns editing the group's poetry magazine *Tads*. One of the Dads was George Stanley, now the oldest important poet in the city of Vancouver. Stanley's most pervasive theme has been the effort to understand one's place, one's use in the physical community one inhabits — first San Francisco, then Vancouver, then Terrace, finally

Vancouver again. Over the years, he has written poems that detail Vancouver stuff, workmen in warehouse, beer parlours, rain on eyeglasses. In the twenty-first century he has been writing a major work called *Vancouver: A Poem*. For a moment let us posit that the voice in the poem is the author's voice. If "Birney" and "Marlatt" and "Knighton" are walkers of the city, "George Stanley" is a bus rider. Usually we read about actual things and events in or outside the buses, which latter are identified. But you remember that the city of Vancouver has never been able to shake off the French poets. So one day George Stanley sees or imagines one on the 99 B-Line bus:

> The reek of wet clothing, the growl of the diesel
> over the fast pulse of its idle
> (like the muffled roar of a captive giant),
> then suddenly, all around, crows cawing.
>
> What is all this to Verlaine, who sits quietly
> in a side seat, the unread *Province* in his lap,
> transported by vision? — a white form,
> a sweet, insistent voice addressing him,
> while he, in response, murmurs the syllables
> of a Name whose cadence quells the bus's rumble.

When I first read the first volume of the poem, I thought that I was reading an attractive 124-page recording of the ordinary life, a championing of diurnal poetry. The volume ends with an image of pensioners kicking their way through autumn leaves, and these little words:

> The mind is this street
> only the interiors
> around it
> arranged
> differently

How much further, I thought, could one be from Shelley's mountain?

But Stanley's poem begins with "his" reading William Carlos Williams on the 210 bus; we catch the poet at the moment, figuring out how to write a city's poem, telling us that it would be a good idea to read *Paterson* as a lead-in. I love this. It is not literary allusion as in Birney, nor is it messing around with literary allusion as in Knighton.

It is a big rime, with the reminder that rime focuses, has to focus, on difference. Vancouver rimes with *Paterson*. If we reread *Paterson* we will see what Stanley is doing in *Vancouver*. We will see two differing cities, poems, illuminated in the shadows of one another.

Williams and Stanley took on these cities/poems later in lives of writing and thinking. In either of them we find the poet's mind coming to a realization, then another realization. Not pedestrian thought, either; on a bus, if one is lucky, one sits. And thinks, perhaps tempted by Hume: "the city itself — the mere fact of it — being — thousands of tons of steel & concrete, glass. It's just an image in the eye — it doesn't exist —" but —

It's fun to follow the bus rider's thoughts, and materialize all at once with him when he suddenly knows

>   the city
>   is not unknowable
>   it's real

Vancouver: A Poem is packed with images of the everyday, and it is also the most philosophical of any poem written about that city so far. It is not finished. It shows no sign that it ever will be.

If you wanted to write an essay about the way Vancouver poetry could transport rather than derange the senses, you might want to compare Apollinaire's snow-covered railroad train with Stanley's No. 99 Broadway bus, ride both poems to the end of the line.

Those Young Rimbauds:
A Discussion about Writing and Reading

A while ago I was reading an interview with my (late) lifelong friend, the writer David McFadden, when I spotted a question put to him by Donato Mancini. To no one, because there was no one else in the house, I said, "I wish I could answer that question." After a short silence I said, "Actually, I can. Who's to stop me?" It was not long till I had written a reply, and then I thought, what about some more questions? From here and there. Before you knew it, and about the time I knew it, I fancied I had found a new literary form. Call it the splinterview.

Interviewer: Were you always writing?

George Bowering: To start with, I was always reading. Still am, even with my aching right eye that couldn't see the letters if I closed my other eye. Lying on my belly on the front room floor, reading World War II in the Vancouver *Province*, seeing the black part of Europe getting smaller every week, and islands in the Pacific flying US flags on long poles where there used to be Japanese flags. So that reading — it was pretty close to writing, wasn't it? When I was ten, I carried drugstore pocket books with me when I climbed the hills solo. You could sit on a rock in the shade and look down at the valley full of fruit trees while also paying attention to Max Brand. But you can't really write while hiking. I probably tried it, but I doubt that I got far, not like Jack Kerouac with his little shirt pocket notebooks. Yesterday, though, I opened up an old photo album, and glued inside were clippings I wrote about the photo section for the station newspaper at RCAF Macdonald, where I was working when I was nineteen. Sure, I had written funny stories and funny little plays and the odd light verse when I was in high school. Pop songs that did not get overly pop, though they did make it to a stage or two in a small town. Letters to Bob Broeg, the sports editor of the St. Louis *Post-Dispatch*. It was a small town; what else was I supposed to do? Writing is reading, isn't it?

Int.: When did you start writing poetry?

GB: I think that I was like most people, somehow writing verses when I was a schoolboy. Goofy rimes about teachers and students, corny clichéed quatrains meant to be love ballads, the inevitable limericks, comic parodies of the hit parade, etc. But I do remember the time when I decided to be serious about being a poet. Up to then I would write a poem and leave it somewhere or give it to someone. But at RCAF Macdonald the library was next to the photo section, and that is where I would go after lunch and before work started in the afternoon. That's where I found books by Kenneth Rexroth and William Carlos Williams — in the middle of snow-swept Manitoba! I was writing very bad short stories, and starting to write love poems to specific subjects of my affection. At the age of twenty-one I left the air force and soon enrolled at the University of British Columbia. I had got myself a ring binder and a three-hole punch, and started typing and saving my poems, starting with the pretentious lyrics written to my girlfriend, who would later ditch me for an Olympic oarsman with muscles and a future. I was orderly, numbering and dating my poems, and when the time eventually came, noting the details of their publication. Another question is "why did you start writing poetry?" That's a tough one. I'd probably say, "Doesn't everyone?"

Int.: How did you learn your craft? There are all these writers' workshops now ...

GB: Yes, that's where they call poetry "your craft." Well, a very small portion of my learning happened in the writing classes (at least they had the sense not to call it "creative" writing) at the University of British Columbia in the late fifties. In your interview with Margaret Atwood, she maintained that there weren't any writing workshops for Canadians back then. Well, she meant that there weren't any in Toronto — this is a conflation we on the west coast are used to hearing from the centre of Canada. I guess I mainly learned about writing poetry from two practices: reading poetry seriously and reading what poets wrote about poetry. William Butler Yeats said something like, "Talk to me about originality, and I will turn upon you with rage." Robert Duncan admitted that he was a "derivative poet," and even published very good poems that he called "derivations." Shelley happily considered himself to be in a line of poets carrying on Dante's work, not as a believer but as a practitioner. Can you imagine Dante, or Shelley, conducting a creative writing workshop? Shelley figured out a lot of things for you, stuff the student on the nearby chair hasn't begun to think about. I have sat in a few workshops. One: I didn't think they resembled a furniture workshop. Two: a lot of time was taken up by a student saying he liked such and such in another student's poem. A class in which newbies tell everyone else what they like?

Int.: How much of a book is in your mind before you start?

GB: That varies a lot, depending on what kind of book I'm hoping to write. Before thinking about the novel *Caprice*, I happened to read a history of Kamloops and a late nineteenth-century story about a USAmerican who shot a French-Canadian ranch hand to death over a bottle of whisky. Of course, I wanted someone to avenge that murder. Then I remembered reading something about the western novel, its conventions and forms and plots. One main plot is the revenge story. You know the movie starring Randolph Scott, the best western star of all time, riding down the bad men who killed his wife? Okay, I said to myself, I have the back story, but because this will be a novel, I have nothing else. I did know that I wanted the US western as a foil (I had read hundreds of them as a teenager), and that the Canadian one would turn it upside down. The lone rider on the revenge trail would be a woman poet from Quebec, and the schoolteacher would be a man, and so on. The Canadian law rather than the lone rider would eventually take care of the bad guys, and so on. I had a lot of fun writing and reading this one. So there's a book for which I made a lot of notes, suggesting that the teacher's love would ride off into the sunrise, for example. Using a lucky accident to slip an old book of poems I owned into the story. Having the last scene orchestrated by my favourite French poet, whose most famous poem was turned into a great tone poem by Debussy while my heroine was riding our hills. A British book reviewer saw this and said so in a Colorado critical journal.

Int.: How much do you revise your work?

GB: A lot less than does Mike Ondaatje, and less frequently than Earle Birney did. Birney's poems got reprinted a lot, and they were different every time, including the time he removed all punctuation marks and replaced them with spaces. I have just looked at a page of handwritten prose for a book I'm writing, and there I saw about three lines scored through, and maybe ten words entered by way of little circumflex-like things, and wouldn't you know it? I have just made some alterations in this paragraph while I convert it from handwriting to type. When I come to typing pages, I change some words, either for accuracy or sound, and either add or subtract commas. While writing, I am in a way hooked up emotionally, listening to the music, whether verse or prose, so that any question of accuracy will apply to rhythm and rime as much as to vocabulary. Sometimes, when I read that some author claims to revise extensively, I think that he's just trying to escape accusations of laziness or loose-mindedness. All right, I do like the story that Hemingway wrote those forty versions of the last page of *A Farewell to Arms*. But here's what I will bet: I will bet that the 39 discarded pages are really good reading. I don't know — are revisions the same things as corrections? Is it a question of getting it right or finding something more interesting? Some of my favourite revisions have been accidental.

Int.: How do you know when to stop working?

GB: Here's something that happens quite often: I have been working on a text that takes several days of sitting — for example, a short story. I sit and open it up and read it, for maybe the eighth time. It comes to me that it's already ended, at least for this draft. Why does this happen? Who knows? Maybe this is a kind of proof of my usual contention that writing and reading are the same thing. Other writers have said that you don't finish but only abandon a poem or fiction. Some poets seem never to finish a poem. Earle Birney, as I have mentioned, emended his poems every time they were republished. I have heard of a writer who writes his last sentence first, then writes toward it. Robert Frost's poems seem to have happened that way. As if the poem were an illustration of an adage. One could do worse than be a swinger of verses, I suppose. The poet is, as they used to say, in control of his materials. What an unhappy situation! You can see the wise old heads bobbing. How true. Life's like that. To return to your question: I look to the poem and bend my ear to find out when to lay down my V5 Pilot Hi-tecpoint 0.5. But I have heard of the poet who uses his pen to make changes to his poems as they appear in the books on his friends' shelves.

Int.: **What are your main influences in your writing?**

GB: My father Ewart's terseness and accuracy in his talking. The dry brown grass and hills of the Okanagan valley, and the shining lakes and dark green orchards that used to punctuate its length on the Canadian side. My feeling of inferiority treated with my secret feeling of superiority, of specialness. Writers such as Robert Kroetsch and Samuel Beckett, who know that looking humorously at human beings and their incapabilities is the way to witness and ameliorate our dreadful tragedy. I don't think of all these things as influences. A river, for instance, is kind of passive about what water flows into it. I am more like the magpie that critics have compared me with.

Here's how writing is reading. This bird spies something shiny, and next thing you know it's become part of whatever's going on in her nest. But you know what? When I hear one of my riffs in someone else's poem, I get over being robbed really fast.

But you said "main." I guess the main thing I will try to appropriate or imitate is a sign of respect for the language, respect shown in some cases by laughter, tickled or horrified. To look at this situation from the other angle, I'd say that if you regard a piece of your own writing and recognize something that is truly yourself, that shows signs of originality, that just might be the best way you ever expressed yourself — scratch it out; or better yet, throw out that piece of writing.

Int.: Is there a sculptor, philosopher, musician, painter or any other type of artist outside the world of poetry and fiction who has inspired your work in a concrete way at some point or other?

GB: I don't think that I can settle on any "concrete" way. I have been a fan, at least, of a number of such people: James Dean, John Coltrane, David Hume, Betty Carter, Barbara Pentland, and José Luis Cuevas, for examples. I have had real friends in the other arts, artists that somehow share an esthetic with me, especially the painters Greg Curnoe, Roy Kiyooka, Brian Fisher, Charlie Pachter, Gordon Payne and Pierre Coupey. All those guys have pictures on my walls, and I played ball with two of them. Inspiration is the business of the muses, of course, and it is related to your age and your "career" curve. When I was a tyro poet, say twenty-one years old, I was breathless about Paul

Klee and Paul Desmond; now, not so much. Oh, I wish you hadn't made me think of breathing concrete! In any case, I know that there are ways of thinking that cross from discipline to discipline, Gertrude Stein doing with words on paper what the Cubists had done with marks on canvas, for example. But my material is the English language and bits of others. I may get a feeling or a direction from a painting or a quartet, but I breathe where the words are. It is interesting that you propose philosophers among the artists. A nimbleness among ideas does kind of seem like something the dancer or poet or ear-bearing fiction writer might share. I have heard my poems set to music and portrayed on film and incorporated in wall art, and if not inspired, I was made happy.

Int.: You can't labour your way into being a poet, can you?

GB: You aren't likely to get there by hard work, but I don't want to sound as if I am in favour of all the stuff I see by people who think you can just be poetic and put your "feelings" down on paper, or stand in a "spoken word" bar and recite how much you suffered because of terrible parents, cruel teachers and schoolyard bullies. Speaking platitudes in a tailored voice to an undemanding audience just means that you can't belabour your way into being a poet, either. I don't know what happens to turn a kid toward poetry, who or what turned on that switch. Here's something I regret: the young poets I knew who had a great ear and a lovely sensibility, those people whose names are still in early copies of our poetry magazines, but who decided to demolish houses, build ashrams overseas or give themselves to a life of drugs in the morning. I look at all the unambitious inattentive stuff in the magazines in our time, and I so much wish those young Rimbauds had kept it up. I like one word that is sometimes used about this subject: "gifted." I am so happy that some spirit gave Keats his gift and that Keats learned to transfer it in his way to us. Labour? No. A gracious spirit sends us a line for free because we have learned as much as we could, and then in thankfulness, with human heart and hopeful ear we try to make the rest of the poem live up to her gift.

Int.: An important part of your work is poetry. What attracts you to writing poetry and what has it taught you?

GB: I started off, as most do, I would guess, as a lyric poet, though I didn't know the term at the time, because you could, if you were lucky, sit anywhere and get the whole thing down in one go. In that way, it was a lot like writing jokes for stand-up comedy (though that term wasn't used back then). Maybe that's why most of my favourite prose writers are comic, like that joker Samuel Beckett. Or listen to some of Ed Dorn's little *Abhorrences* and the poems in *Hello, La Jolla*, poems he wrote while driving the San Diego Freeway. "Dumb fucks in pickup trucks," etc. If I'm working on a long prose piece, a novel, for example, I like the romance of sitting in front of a keyboard every day, the pile of paper getting higher and higher. Being able to jot a few lines on the inside cover of a paperback attracts me to poetry. Has writing poetry taught me anything? Well, it took many years, but I learned to get away from the fake present tense. You can learn how to write by reading, as everyone tells the rookies, and you can learn to read by writing, as Bowering tells the tads. I sat down and typed

Sheila Watson's great novel *The Double Hook*, and learned more than I had learned in all the previous times I had read it. I haven't had the nerve to do a similar thing with *The Cantos*, but I have typed or handwritten a lot of other poems I hadn't written. Give it a try with Gerard Manley Hopkins.

Int.: To what extent do you think a poet's writing is a compost of the materials he's read?

GB: Not counting other people's work he might have typed out, I guess? "Milton! thou should'st be living at this hour"? Well, he was. He still is. Writing, say poetry, is a world, and we enter it by reading or writing, which are parts of the same thing, as I have said, I think. It's been pointed out to me that a lot of my writing has been rewriting or otherwise responding to other writers and what they have left us. Yes, that's right. I have had Shakespeare, Homer, Rilke, Stein and Keats whispering in my skull. I'm never going to say the last word on anything, and neither will anyone else. Joyce did not correct Homer, and he did not copy him. One of the proudest moments of my life was the time I read my daughter's comic rewriting of one of my stories. I think that your figure "compost" is a lot better than "influence." Influence, I never tire of pointing out, suggests a creek contributing to a river. A writer's writing, even if he believes in the subconscious, is his way of reading the language that surrounds him. He is, you might say, doing his share of the big job we are all doing. I guess a lot of bad writing could be referred to as garbage, but in 1802 William Wordsworth was composting in his romantic head. And he too is living at this hour.

Int.: How do you go about titling a poem?

GB: It just comes to me. Usually soon after I finish writing the first draft of the poem. Here is another place or time when or where writing is another term for something called reading. Ismael Reed said writin' is fightin', but for me writin' is readin'. You tired of hearing that? I am reading the words I am inking this page with right now. Sometimes the title comes quickly, as the Holy Ghost did to my grandfather, who was writing the end of his life. *Revelation* 22:20. Sometimes you see a title-like phrase in the middle of the poem, and there you are! Sometimes you sit and wait, and eventually the title comes, and you wonder: what? Why is that the title? For a certain kind of poem or poem sequence you go to an old text by a poet who is "still living at this hour", and find a good phrase therein, thus giving your readers a semi-veiled hint. On a very few occasions someone in some fashion has assigned a subject or title, and you have it imposed, a directive that produces a title. If you believe in the subconscious you can even say that she assigns it. My poem "The Neonate" was begun with the title given to me, and I can't remember who gave it. I hate it when cutesy-wootsy titles become a fad. A couple years ago every book published by a Victoria, BC, writer had a title something like *Loving Those who Drive the Nails Deep*. Maybe we should just title poems the way we name dogs.

Int.: Could you comment on the importance of rime in poetry?

GB: Think of "The Rime of the Ancient Mariner." Or "Rhymes of a Rolling Stone." Or "The Structure of Rime."

Sometimes "rime" is another word for "poetry." I wouldn't, as a rule, go that far, but I would certainly go in that direction. All poems do rime. Sometimes a lot. Sometimes not to any discernible advantage. Did you think that when some utterance you've made is said to be with neither rime nor reason, you were supposed to croon at the moon? There are, yes, a lot of people who think that rime is obliged to happen at the end of the line. Or they mention "interior" rime, as if sounds had insides and outsides. I guess it was a lot of fun making up "slant rime" and "near rime" and "off rime," and getting school kids to remember which is which. But did they have to tell those kids that some poetry is "unrimed?" Poets work with all the possibilities of sound. There is no such thing as "half rime." Robert Duncan posited a "scale of resemblances," so that we might associate that moon with a sweet tune, a bit less with a mirror, hardly at all with a waste basket. Rime helps a reader find her way, as the colour of the ground leads us to water. If you would like to take a ride on rime, read aloud H.D.'s evocative "Oread." I'll bet that a person who doesn't read English would still enjoy hearing your reading.

Int.: Do you think poets choose to become poets — or does poetry choose them?

GB: For a long time I have been trying to decide whether that is a woo-woo question. Let's just say I don't think I ever chose to be a poet. I don't remember thinking that there was a choice of things to be, though there were school notions and parent notions and popular magazine quiz notions that played with such a prospect. I wanted to be a crime fighter. Then I wanted to be a sports writer.

I didn't fight a lot of crime, but I reported baseball and basketball games for two newspapers when I was a schoolboy. My first nationally published poems were in a hockey magazine. Maybe some people do choose to be poets, not that the choice turns out very well, sometimes. I guess I wanted to be a writer, and my first success of sorts was with poems. I think it's easier to get published with poems because there's a pretty broad tolerance as to what is any good in poetry. As to whether poetry chooses individuals to help write it — I can't imagine that poetry has that kind of agency, though it may seem tempting or enjoyable to think that way, to seem mysterious as befits a poet. But I do think that anyone who hopes to be a serious poet should serve the language, never to use it. To see and hear its demands, not his own or his publisher's or his reader's.

Int.: Poetry is a really hard sell for a lot of people. What, if any, argument do you have for people who are intimidated by poetry?

GB: I often hear that people are intimidated by poetry, including kids in school. If I am among people outside the poetry world I see some becoming embarrassed around me because they think they might be failing by not getting it or even liking to be around it. People get that way when they are introduced to an opera baritone, I'll bet. Part of me likes the thought of such intimidation, because one does want to do something that matters, and danger matters. But really, if you have little children, you know that children love song and rime. They get introduced to wit in kids' books that rime. Why not encourage it as a lifelong activity? It seems as if just about all people, when they get their backs to the wall, resort to making up end-riming poetry. They write obituaries made of verses when someone in their family dies. When some official searches the pockets of soldiers killed in battle, they often find folded paper bearing handwritten poems. I know that a lot of people shy away from poetry, but I also know people who start every day by reading a poem. When my mother turned a hundred she recited Wordsworth's "I wandered lonely as a cloud," which she was told to memorize in high school (though she thought at a hundred that she was reciting Longfellow). She was far from intimidated; imagine, that poem stayed with her for nearly a century!

Int.: I take it that you feel the connections between you and the "Black Mountain School" are overblown.

GB: Starting in the late sixties, a lot of conservative and/or lazy academics, mainly English professors at eastern Canadian universities, started referring to me and Fred Wah and Daphne Marlatt, etc., as "Black Mountain Poets." They knew nothing about Black Mountain, and very little about poetry. A person had to put up with a lot of nuisance, for instance the well-known Canadian Literature "scholar" at a Montreal university who asked me just where in British Columbia Black Mountain is. I told her it was a popular ski resort just north of Vancouver, where the poets were known to recite their works on the slopes and in the ski lodge. Later, I found out that there is a Black Mountain peak somewhere in the northern Okanagan valley.

I don't know where all this dopiness began. Yes, during our school days some of us west coast poetry kids assiduously read Charles Olson and Robert Creeley, and we dropped their names whenever we could. But though Olson was the last rector of the experimental Black Mountain College in the unsnowy hills of western North Carolina, I don't know of any Canadian writer who ever went there. Irving Layton, who was listed as a contributing editor of the Spain-based *Black Mountain Review*, joined the know-nothing crowd who denounced us every chance he got. As for me, I'm from the southern Okanagan valley. All our mountains are brown.

Int.: What happens when you perform your work in front of an audience? What's the necessity of reading in your voice in time?

GB: You know, when I was a youngster there was a canard among academics that poets were notoriously the worst readers of their own work. I have been to a great many poetry readings, and I must report that any serious poet writes for his voice. Once on the radio I heard Richard Burton the actor reading poems by John Donne. Now, Donne was a conflicted horny man of God, and he explored that conflict in his poems — I mean in the very syntax and punctuation of his poems. Richard Burton of the lovely voice just happily sailed his way through the lines, beautiful, not a problem in the world. Might as well get Mary Poppins to read Allen Ginsberg's "Howl" to the kiddies. For heaven's sake, the poem on the page is there to tell us what it sounds like coming out of the poet's mouth. When we were all newbies Lionel Kearns used to come to the podium with a pencil, with which he would emend any errors he noticed in the written text's version of his poem. Over the years I have heard some inferior voicings of poetry, but that was usually a result of some unfortunate poet's dreadful speaking voice to begin with. You don't write a poem and then get someone to elocute it. You write your voicing. If you can't pronounce the word "chthonic", don't write it.

Int.: Some authors feel characters take on "a life of their own" during the writing process. Do you agree with this, or is a writer always in control?

GB: Actually, I suppose that I have to say no to both sides of the question. I have said that a fiction writer can arrange it so that a big iron safe will fall from the sky and squash his character when his character steps outside his building. Let's see him take on a life of his own then! But at the same time I am chary of the writer's being in total control. I think (and notice that I do not make use of that verb "feel") that the author should partly give up control, not to his character but to the language and its demands. Hand over control, I say, to see what surprises might be afforded you in the composition of this story. Poetry has a lot to teach in regard to this situation. If the poet lays down his resistance, the sound his poem has made so far will offer music and promote imagery for the rest of the poem. Sound can shape events in fiction, too. Writers who favour a Freudian model, as so many did in the twentieth century, might counsel a weakening of the ego in the search for the real in imaginative prose. Some writers might go for a kind of Buddhist surrender. If you think that fiction can be a stream-of-consciousness, why not keep your senses open and float downstream? No, my "character" does not have a life of his own, but then neither do I. I pay attention when the muse says, "listen!" I know what young novelists mean when they say that their characters have taken over, but it sounds to me a little too much like God bestowing free will, and I say that writers are not God.

Int.: Laughter seems to give us a temporary release from our egos. Is that one of the reasons humour has been such a key element in your work?

GB: Maybe that's why I haven't been translated much into German. Well, I have noticed that the authors I like and imitate so much, whether we call them post-modern or not, are humorous. But what about the great modernists — Camus, H.D., Pound, Eliot? A lot of the great modernists such as those people never crack a joke, and probably don't get them when someone else does. Can you imagine what Woody Allen might have said when the huge one-eyed monster in the cave asked him who he was? A few of the modernist crowd make jokes — Joyce and Beckett, for instances. Their excuse is that they are Irish. The closest Eliot comes is irony, and it is fueled by snobbery. Everyone in the nineteenth century was earnest. Dickens, Hardy, Melville, Stendhal. I don't recall those people or their characters escaping their egos so much. But most of my favourite writers are funny — Beckett again, Flann O'Brien, Vonnegut, M.A.C. Farrant, Kroetsch. The great modernists, as I said, knew irony. Well, that's better than the earnestness of Robert Frost. As for me, I like all sorts of humour. My favourite US movie of recent decades is *Ishtar*. The US intelligence organizations started a campaign to make people think that *Ishtar* is the standard-bearer for bad movies. It happens that in the movie we see that the US supports the dictator of an African country, so a couple of songwriters use hand-held weapons to bring down the US air force that is fighting against the freedom-fighters. Now *that's* funny.

Int.: Which of your characters do you feel more connected to? Why?

GB: First, let me say in reply to another question and this one, that I would just as soon not refer to them as "characters." Characters are in a way symbols, like runes, something to figure out. People develop characteristics, and that is how we understand them. I prefer "figures," a term that we may usefully compare with figures in paintings and music and dance, even architecture. Figures, your dictionary will tell you, are shapes given to things. Given, let us say, by the artist. I have been in too many literature classes in which the professors talk about Hester Prynne or Duddy Kravitz as if they were real people you might meet in the street or the woods. When you start seeing them that way you can start psychoanalyzing them and checking out their motives, etc., rather than regarding them as constructions by their authors. I have been told by readers that certain of my inventions "stepped right off the page" and into their lives. No. Those people are not giving themselves enough credit for the work they have done as readers, and while you are at it, I could use a little credit, too. What I gave you were words and sentences, and if we are both doing our jobs well enough, we imagine a world. And you know well that when a filmmaker finishes, the movie is a third version — his; it does not look like the one you saw in your head, nor like the one in mine.

Int.: Do you approach the short story differently than

the novel?

GB: In reading them, yes. Maybe less so in writing them. But here is something: it is just as true of the story as it is of the novel — there are all kinds of them. The old realists used to ask of themselves: what was that man like? Or what was it like in that town? As for me, I am more likely to ask: I wonder whether I could get away with doing this? It is true that when sentenced to writing a novel you will say that this led to that and then that led in turn to this other. Usually, in a story you say that led to this and now here we are. While writing a novel you might follow some animal down a hole, but in a story you know that if you do that you'll wind up in another story, so you'd better throw away the one you started with. The most obvious difference is that you will spend seven years on a novel, so you'd better not be too old, and if you're not, you might as well settle in. But Hemingway once wrote three stories in one day. I rewrote one of them, and then quit for the week. Questions such as yours are often approached in high school literature classes and college creative writing classes. Here is a piece of advice I gave myself in high school, and continued listening to in college: whatever truths or procedures are said to pertain to writing fiction or poetry I am going to question and try to contradict. In school I was told that a noun was the name of a person, place or thing. I replied that in choosing between white paint and blue for my wall I chose the blue. The teacher said that "paint" was understood. I said, I'm going somewhere where we study the words we use, not the ones we don't use.

Int.: Politics is in the air at the moment. How does it

manifest itself in your writing?

GB: I try to write politics as I write any other thing, love, etc. When I was young, I tried to write political poems loudly, capital letters and exclamation points and all that. Imperative sentences, pronouns, you know what. Turned out some terrible things; they were almost as bad as Neruda's paean to Stalin. It should not take long to learn that a bad communist poem is as bad as a bad fascist poem. But you know, the best political poet was Shelley, who was also the best philosophical poet, the best nature poet, the best love poet, etc. The mistake that a lot of everyday rimesters make is to set poems at the *service* of something — advertising, patriotism, charity, someone's birthday. You're an idiot if you would *use* poetry. I have even heard poetry described as a *tool* to accomplish something. Shelley knew better: he wrote "Rarely, rarely comest thou, Spirit of Delight!" Poetry is older, more intelligent, more powerful and better looking than anyone else in the room. Anyone who believes that he can create a masterpiece has got his directions in reverse. Poetry and politics were perhaps born around the same time, but politics were invented because something was not so good and needed fixing. Poetry is where you want to go, not the way you get there.

Int.: What did getting the Order of Canada mean to you?

GB: You don't often see me wearing the pin, but I always notice when someone else does, on TV or in real life. I guess I would wear it more often if I wore a jacket with a lapel more often, but I am a retired old softy who likes to get through his days in pyjamas. When they refer to the OC as an honour, I agree. I feel greatly honoured. Not that I don't think I deserve it. For one thing, it means that someone outside the writing racket is impressed. It makes up for the fact that no one in my family ever gave a hoot about any successes I might have as a writer. I remember that when I got the Governor General's Award the second time, my mum said a little girl in her home town did, too. I think she saw a TV news clip depicting the Governor General pinning a medal of bravery on a young local girl. I've kept an even keel, though. When I won my first Governor General's Award, my colleagues in the English department at Sir George Williams University in Montreal denied me a raise because as far as they were aware, I hadn't published anything. I don't do all that well in small towns, either. In my home town, Oliver, BC, which I have written many pages about, it has never been possible to buy one of my books. I have done three readings at the library in Oliver over the years. One of them was attended by one of my sister's daughters. No one else in my family, which lives in and around Oliver, has ever come to hear me read.

Int.: What do you listen to?

GB: My heart, that poor mistreated muscle. The voice of unreason. The mockingbird. Jean's directives dressed in the raiment of good counsel. All of the above. But I know that you mean music and the like. We have the fortune of listening to online radio, with speakers all over the condo, as well as a large collection of vinyl (45's and LPs) and tape cassettes and CDs and those other things. But mostly I listen to radio music. In the mornings it's classical, chamber music if I'm lucky, Brahms if I'm being picky. In the evening it's jazz, most often from a station in Cartagena. They seem to have about fifteen records, but luckily a couple of them are by John Coltrane. When I first bought this online radio service I would seek out and play a Swiss station that played post-Coltrane free jazz, my favourite. But they have disappeared, and now I may hear Coltrane here and there, but it's always the softer stuff, no honk, no screech, and no Ornette, no Giuseppe Logan. So I dial carefully and settle for okay. If I have a strong enough yen, I go through my vinyl for some Paul Bley, some Archie Shepp, some Sun Ra, some Art Ensemble of Chicago. I listen to singers, too. I always get the frightened shivers when I play one of my many Nina Simone albums. I love Betty Carter and Dinah Washington and Etta James and Dee Dee Bridgewater and Koko Taylor. If you want me to listen to men singing, let them be Nat Cole or Ray Charles or the Stylistics.

The Proust Questionnaire (late nineteenth-century parlour game):

Int.: Earliest memory of reading. Of writing.

GB: The Vancouver *Province*, spread on the front room floor in Peachland, BC, I am keeping track of the war in Europe. Copying the big flashcards being held by my grade one teacher in Greenwood, BC.

Int.: When you knew you'd be a writer.

GB: When I first read Grantland Rice.

Int.: Occupation you would have chosen other than literature.

GB: Sports writer.

Int.: Favourite pastime.

GB: *The New York Times* crossword. In ink.

Int.: Favourite writer.

GB: Robert Kroetsch. Just beats out H.D.

Int.: Favourite artist and musician/composer.

GB: Paul Cézanne and Paul Bley.

Int.: Favourite colour, flower, and bird.

GB: Yellow, yellow roses, and goldfinch.

Int.: Favourite food and drink.

GB: Meatloaf and vanilla milkshake.

Int.: Favourite smell and sound.

GB: Lemon and John Coltrane's tenor.

Int.: Favourite environment or landscape.

GB: Desert-like Okanagan valley.

Int.: Favourite weather or season.

GB: A sunny spring day.

Int.: Favourite expression, catchphrase, proverb or word.

GB: Favourite word is "chicken."

Int.: Best quality.

GB: Fairness, mixed with humour.

Int.: Worst flaw.

GB: Hesitancy.

Int.: Ideal place to live.

GB: Ideals exist only in the regretful mind.

Int.: One wish.

GB: Longevity.

Int.: Aspiration before you die.

GB: To be loved by everyone.

Int.: To me writing is —

GB: — the reason for everything else.

Notes on Sources

"Were you always writing?", Jeanne McCulloch and Mona Simpson int. Alice Munro, *The Paris Review* 131, Summer 1994.

"When did you start writing poetry?", Michael Newman int. W.H. Auden, *The Paris Review* 47, Spring 1974.

"How did you learn your craft? There are all these writers' workshops now . . .", Shannon Hengen and Joyce Meier int. Margaret Atwood, *Iowa Journal of Literary Studies* Vol. 7, Issue 1, 1986.

"How much of a book is in your mind before you start?", Hermione Lee int. Philip Roth, *The Paris Review* 93, Fall 1984.

"How much do you revise your work?", Mary Jane Fortunato, Lucille Medwick and Susan Bowe int. Allen Ginsberg, *The New York Quarterly*, Issue 6, Spring 1971.

"How do you know when to stop working?", Willem Dafoe int. Michael Ondaatje, *Bomb*, January 1, 1997.

"What are your main influences in your writing?", Christie Allarie int. Rudy Wiebe, Writers' Guild of Alberta website, 2015.

"Is there a fiction writer, philosopher, musician, painter or any other type of artist outside the world of poetry who has inspired your work in a concrete way at some point or other?", Lynn Coady int. Erín Moure, CBC, May 7, 2017.

"You can't labour your way into being a poet, can you?", Choire Sicha int. Ursula K Le Guin, *Interview*, Sept. 4, 2015.

"One important part of your work is poetry. What attracts you to writing poetry and what has it taught you?", Jack Crouch int. Priscilla Uppal, *The Malahat Review* website, 2014.

"To what extent do you think a poet's writing is a compost of the materials he's read?", Donato Mancini int. David W. McFadden, *Causal Talk: interviews with four poets*, Ottawa, above/ground press, 2004.

"How do you go about titling a poem?", Adam Fitzgerald int. John Ashbery, *Interview*, April 20, 2015.

"Could you comment on the importance of rime in poetry?", Ajmer Rode int. Marilyn Bowering, *South Asian Ensemble* 1.1, Autumn 2009.

"Do you think poets choose to become poets — or does poetry choose them?", Kate Kellaway int. Anne Carson, *The Guardian*, Oct. 30, 2016.

"Poetry is a really hard sell for a lot of people. What, if any, argument do you have for people who are intimidated by poetry?", Corina Milic int. Susan Musgrave, *Feathertale Review*, Feb. 15, 2016.

"I take it that you feel the connections made between you and the 'Black Mountain School' are overblown.", Tandy Sturgeon int. Ed Dorn, *Contemporary Literature*, Vol. 27, No. 1, Spring, 1986.

"What happens when you perform your work in front of an audience? What's the necessity of reading in your voice in time?",

Nick Sturm int. Alice Notley, Poetry Society of America, n.d. poetrysociety.org/features

"Some authors feel characters take on a 'life of their own' during the writing process. Do you agree with this, or is a writer always in control?", Grace O'Connell int. Leon Rooke, *Open Book*, Sept. 19, 2016.

"Laughter seems to give us a temporary release from our egos. Is that one of the reasons humour has been such a key element in your work?", Donato Mancini int. David W. McFadden, *Interviews With Four Poets*, Ottawa, 2004.

"Which of your characters do you feel more connected to? Why?", Lucy Hannau int. Isabel Allende, *BookBrowse*, December 2012.

"Do you approach the short story differently than the novel?", Gail Anderson-Dargatz int. Jack Hodgins for her website, Summer, 2007.

"Politics is in the air at the moment. How does it manifest itself in your writing?", Leverett Smith int. Michael Rumaker, *Rain Taxi*, Spring, 2009.

"What did getting the Order of Canada mean to you?", Jane Stevenson int. Catherine O'Hara, *Vancouver Sun*, January 8, 2019.

"What do you listen to?", Anjelica Huston int. Leonard Cohen, *Interview*, November, 1995.

Acknowledgments

The author thanks the editors of the following publications and electronic media, where many of these pieces were originally published: *Canada Writes*, CBC One (How I Wrote *Mirror on the Floor*), *Canadian Poetry* (Apollinaire and Vancouver), *The Capilano Review* blog (Collections; Kroetsch Listens; Hooray, Difficulty!), CBC and National Public Radio (The Holy Life of the Intellect), *Dooney's Cafe* (Pages I Have Trouble With 3: Grappa; The Objects of My Affection), *The Globe & Mail* (Fitz; He's Up Again!), The Grreat Canadian Writers' Craft Interview, Open Book, Toronto (Six Answers for Rebecca Tuck, Who Asked About Greg Curnoe and Me), *A Thousand Words*, Alex Waterhouse-Hayward's blog (Look at That) and *The Vancouver Sun* (Seems Like Happiness).

He Gets Better Every Year was originally published as the introduction to *if wants to be the same as is: Essential Poems of David Bromige*, ed. Jack Krick, Bob Perelman, and Ron Silliman (New Star Books, 2017).

Letters from Mike originally appeared in *My Faculties at Large*, by Michael Matthews (Duncan, Outlaw Editions, 2013). Notes on "I Like Summer" was written for *The Revolving City: 51 Poems and the Stories Behind Them*, ed. by Wayde Compton and Renee Sarojini Saklikar (Anvil Press, 2015).

Index

Abhorrences, 145
Absalom, Absalom!, 101
Acorn, Milton, 45, 123–24
Adiga, Aravind, 101
"Adonais," 97
Aiken, Conrad, 120
Air Canada, 7–8
Allen, Donald, 41, 75
Allen, Woody, 153
American Testament, 79–80
Angel, Leonard, 41
Apollinaire, Guillaume, 114–16, 119, 136
archives, 51–55, 91, 111
Art Ensemble of Chicago, 158
arts, government funding for, 6, 53–55
Ashbery, John, 35
"As Long As Purgatory Rimes With Virtue," 79–80
"A Step this Side of Salvation," 3
Atwood, Margaret, 60, 95, 101, 108, 139
Audain, Michael, 9
Avasilichioaei, Oana, 4–5
Avison, Margaret, 76
Ayler, Albert, 47

Bach, J.S., 52
Baird, Irene, 122
Baird, Jean, 20, 49, 61, 63–65, 157
Barker, George, 75
Barre du jour, La, 106
baseball, 13, 34, 40, 42, 49, 93, 109, 118–19, 143, 149
Battle of Algiers (movie), 11–12

Beckett, Samuel, 40, 142, 145, 153
"Bed and Breakfast," 44
Beethoven, Ludwig van, 9–10, 29
Bennett, Avie, 22
Bernstein, Charles, 78
Birney, Earle, 45, 121–22, 127–29, 130, 131, 134, 141, 142
Black Mountain School, 150–51
Black Sparrow Press, 78
Blaser, Robin, 118
Bley, Paul, 158, 159
Blonds on Bikes, 48
Bowering, Angela, 97
Bowering, Ewart, 142
Bowering, George: in air force, 66, 74, 138; childhood, 2, 34, 66, 73, 92–95, 112–14, 137–38, 158; Order of Canada, 156–57; Parliamentary Poet Laureate, 51; photo, 28; publishing, 38, 39, 40, 51, 81–82, 91, 103, 138–39 (*see also specific titles*); reading lists, 92, 94–96; university student, 37–39, 47, 66–68, 69, 73, 75–76, 96–97, 99, 102, 138–39
Bowering, Thea, 50, 130, 146
Bowering fonds, 51–52, 91
Boxer, Avi, 106
Boyle, John, 48
Brahms, Johannes, 157
Brainard, Joe, 49
Breton, André, 117–18
Brides of the Stream, 44
Bridge, The, 66
Bridgewater, Dee Dee, 158

INDEX

Brimsek, Frank, 93
Broeg, Bob, 138
Bromige, David, 40, 73–74, 75–80
Brossard, Nicole, 85, 106
Browne, Colin, 41
Buddhism, 14, 152
Burton, Richard, 151

Calvino, Italo, 24
Camus, Albert, 153
Canadian Literature, 74
Cantos, The, 32, 48, 146
Capilano Review, The, 9
Caprice, 140
Carr, Emily, 122
Carter, Betty, 143, 158
Carver, Raymond, 31
Cataract, 106
Catch, 39
Catcher in the Rye, 112
Cavalcanti, Guido, 67
Cendrars, Blaise, 116–17, 119
Cézanne, Paul, 159
Charenton, 31
Charles, Ray, 158
"Christ Walks In This Infernal District Too," 119–20, 126
Circle Game, The, 108
Cleaver, Eldridge, 11
Cloud Atlas, 23–24
Coach House Press, 26, 45, 98, 127
Cohen, Leonard, 3, 27, 61–65, 106
Cole, Nat King, 158
Coleman, Ornette, 64, 158
Coleman, Victor, 48
Collins, Phil, 9
Coltrane, John, 9, 18, 29, 143, 158, 159
"Composition as Explanation," 90
Cone, Tom, 41–42
Confidence-Man, The, 101
Conrad, Joseph, 101
Contact Press, 108

Cooley, Dennis, 16
Copithorne, Judith, 40
Corman, Cid, 110
Coupey, Pierre, 143
Crane, Hart, 66
Cream, 62
Creeley, Robert, 50, 67, 76, 91–92, 99, 105, 150
Cuevas, José Luis, 143
Curnoe, Greg, 29, 47–50, 96, 143
Curnoe, Sheila, 50

Davey, Frank, 75
David, Jack, 81
Dawson, David, 69
Dean, James, 143
Deep Truth, The, 100
Delaunay, Robert, 115–16
DeLottinville, Peter, 51–55
Desert Music, The, 17, 66
Desmond, Paul, 144
Deverell, William, 33
Diamond, Neil, 10
Dick, Philip K., 119
Dickens, Charles, 153
"Donna mi prega," 67
Donne, John, 151
"Door, The," 67
Dorn, Ed, 145
Dos Passos, John, 121
Dostoyevsky, Fyodor, 111
Double Hook, The, 21, 145–46
Dream Craters, 45
Dudek, Louis, 3
Duncan, Robert, 67, 75, 76, 78, 109, 139, 148
Dunn, Joe, 109

Each Man's Son, 29
Eco, Umberto, 90, 111
ECW Press, 81
Eggs in There, 49

"Eh You," 3
Eliot, George, 101
Eliot, T.S., 153
Ends of the Earth, The, 78
En Route, 7–8
Escape from the Glue Factory, 43
Euripides, 84

Fanon, Frantz, 11
Farewell to Arms, A, 96, 141
Farkas, Endre, 107
Farrant, M.A.C., 153
"Far West," 116–17
Faulkner, William, 101
Fenollosa, Ernest, 99
Fisher, Brian, 143
Fitzgerald, Judith, 4, 25–27, 61–62
football, 32
42nd Parallel, The, 121
Four Saints in Three Acts, 32
Franklin, John, 30
Fraser, Art, 93
"From Charles Street, Pandemonium," 131–33
Frost, Robert, 4, 68, 113, 142, 153
Frye, Northrop, 101, 102

Gadd, Maxine, 40
Game Misconduct, 42
Gardiner, Earle Stanley, 94
Gathering, The, 77
Gilbert, Gerry, 40, 110
Ginsberg, Allen, 3, 50, 76, 97
Glassco, John, 106
"God's Grandeur," 71
Gold, Artie, 3, 107
Governor General's Award, 15, 157
Greene, Graham, 105, 111
Grenier, Robert, 78
Grosset & Dunlap, 95
Gustafson, Ralph, 106

"Half an Egg on the Lawn," 45–46
Hardy, Thomas, 153
Haselwood, David, 109, 110
Hawkes, John, 107
H.D. (Hilda Doolittle), 67, 96, 123, 148, 153, 159
Heart Does Break, The, 49
Hello, La Jolla, 145
Hemingway, Ernest, 37, 95, 96, 141, 155
Hertz, K.V., 106
hockey, 34, 42, 93, 149
Holland, Eddie, 9
Hollingsworth, Margaret, 40
Homer, 84–85, 146
Hope (BC), 113
Hopkins, Gerard Manley, 67–72, 146
House of Anansi, 101, 108
Howith, Harry, 105
Huckleberry Finn, 89
Hughes, Ted, 91
Hulme, T.E., 99
Hume, David, 126, 131, 143
"Hymn to Intellectual Beauty," 18
Hypocritic Days, The, 105

If on a winter's night a traveller, 24
if wants to be the same as is, 77, 78
"I Like Summer," 34–36
Imago, 48
In the Skin of the Lion, 56–60
Ishtar, 153–54
"I wandered lonely as a cloud," 150

Jalovec, John, 93
James, Etta, 158
James, Henry, 29, 111
Jesus, as windhover, 69–70
Johnson, Pauline, 122
Jones, D.G., 106
Jones, LeRoi, 75
Joyce, James, 84, 146, 153

INDEX

Kantorowicz, Ernst, 75
Kearns, Lionel, 98, 102, 151
Keats, John, 80, 124, 145
Kelly, Robert, 111
Kenner, Hugh, 115
Kerouac, Jack, 37, 97, 137
Kiyooka, Roy, 104, 107, 110, 143
Klee, Paul, 143–44
Klinkowitz, Jerome, 99
Knighton, Ryan, 131–33, 134
Kroetsch, Robert, 7, 15–16, 142, 153, 159

Lambert, Betty, 40
Lane, Patrick, 44, 104, 110
Lane, Red, 49
language: and writing, 1, 76–80, 130, 144, 146, 149; difficulty of, 1, 4–5, 78–80, 130; respect for, 26–27, 65, 113, 143, 149, 152, 155. *See also* translation
Language Poets, 32, 76, 80
Laurence, Margaret, 39, 103
Lawrence, D.H., 32
Layton, Irving, 13, 106, 151
Lazarus, John, 40
Lear, Edward, 119
Levertov, Denise, 76, 99
Library and Archives Canada, 51–55, 91
Liquidities, 129–30
listening, 10, 13, 15–16, 83, 127, 141, 152
lists, 90–92, 111
Literary Disruptions, 99
Livesay, Dorothy, 98, 103–4
locus, 47, 125–26, 127
Logan, Giuseppe, 158
London, Jack, 94
Lovely Lady, The, 32
Love Supreme, A, 18
Loving Those who Drive the Nails Deep, 147
Lowry, Malcolm, 119–21, 126
LSD Leacock, The, 45
Lyttle, Bill, 37, 38

MacEwen, Gwen, 45
Mackintosh, Graham, 110
mail, 19–20
Makse, Joe, 93
Mancini, Donato, 9–10, 137
Marlatt, Daphne, 27, 98, 127, 129–30, 131, 134, 150
Matthews, Karen, 42
Matthews, Mike, 19–20, 22, 44
Maurer, Rolf, 9–10, 96
Maximus Poems, 48
Mayne, Seymour, 106, 110
McClelland & Stewart, 21–22, 38, 39, 103
McFadden, David, 3, 48, 59, 137
McLuhan, Marshall, 102
Measure for Measure, 101
Melville, Herman, 101, 153
Merril, Judith, 94
Middlemarch, 101
Milton, John, 131–32
Mirror on the Floor, 37–39
Mitchell, David, 23–24
Mitchell, Roscoe, 47
"Mont Blanc," 79, 97, 123, 126
Montreal, 96–97, 100, 101, 103–4, 106–7
Moore, Marianne, 75
Morrison, Toni, 78, 105
Moscovitch, Henry, 106
Moure, Erín, 5, 31
Moustache, The, 48, 49
movies, 11–12, 23, 60, 92–93, 140, 153, 154
Munro, Alice, 22
music, 9–10, 17, 18, 47, 48, 50, 61–65, 143–44, 157–58, 159. *See also specific musicians*

Naked Poems, 110
National Library of Canada. *See* Library and Archives Canada
Naylor, Paul, 111
"Nechako Spring Morning," 3

"Neonate, The," 147
Neruda, Pablo, 156
New American Poetry, 1945–1960, The, 41, 75
New Canadian Library, 21
Newlove, John, 40, 110
newspapers, 92
Nichol, bp, 49
Nihilist Spasm Band, 48
Nineteen Eighty-four, 112
No One, 81–82, 84–88, 89
Norris, Ken, 107
Nostromo, 101
"November Walk Near False Creek Mouth," 127–29

objectification, 81–84, 85–87
O'Brien, Flann, 153
October Ferry to Gabriola, 121
"Ode to the West Wind," 71
Odyssey, 84–85
Okanagan, 2
Oliver Chronicle, 38
Olson, Charles, 48, 67, 75, 76, 80, 83, 124, 125–28, 150–51
Olympic Games, Vancouver 2010, 6
Ondaatje, Michael, 56–57, 59–60, 141
On the Road, 111
"Oread," 148
"Ornithology," 17
Ossman, David, 99
"Owl and the Pussycat, The," 119

Pachter, Charlie, 143
Parker, Charlie, 17
Parliamentary Poet Laureate, 51
Partridge, Eric, 82
Paterson, 124–25, 135
Pato, Chus, 31
Paul, St., of Tarsus, 18
Payne, Gordon, 143
Peckham, Morse, 30
Pentland, Barbara, 122, 143

Piccolo Mondo, 73
Pierce, Lorne, 98
Pierre, or The Ambiguities, 100–101
Pitch of Poetry, 78
"Poem Beginning with a Line from Pindar," 67
poetry: allusion, 69–71, 135, 147; collections, 9–10; intimidating, 149–50; and place, 47, 113, 122–27, 133 (*see also* Vancouver: in poetry); publishing, 149; rime, 70, 75, 127, 135, 141, 147–48; theory, 68–69, 71; writing, 3, 4–5, 13, 35–36, 99–100, 115–17. *See also* language; reading; writing; *specific poets*
poetry readings, 151–52
politics, 6, 53–54, 155–56
Pollock, Sharon, 41
Pontecorvo, Gillo, 11–12
Pound, Ezra, 9, 32, 48, 67, 97, 153
Powell's Books, 91
Prism, 74
"Projective Verse," 83, 125
proprioception, 126, 127, 130, 131
Prose Keys to Modern Poetry, 99
Proust Questionnaire, 158–60
Pulos, C.E., 100
Purdy, Al, 45, 104

Ra, Sun, 158
Raven, The, 37, 74
reading: allusion, 56–60; experiencing another mind, 17–18, 79–80, 126–27; imagination, 112, 154; learn by writing, 145–46; novels, 1; poetry, 4–5, 9–10, 13, 25–27, 31, 32–33, 35–36, 68–71, 77–78; and representation, 9–10; same as writing, 13, 141–42, 145–46; takes effort, 4–5, 24, 25–27, 31–33, 69–72, 78–79, 84–86, 88. *See also* language; poetry; writing
Réage, Pauline, 88
Reaney, James, 55

INDEX

Red Shoes, The, 95
Reed, Ismael, 147
Reid, Jamie, 40, 75, 97
Reid, Robert, 109
Rexroth, Kenneth, 138
Rice, Grantland, 158
Rimbaud, Arthur, 131
Ripley, Robert, 94
Roberts, Kevin, 44
Romeo and Juliet, 6
Rosen, Sheldon, 40
Rosenblatt, Joe, 43–46
Roth, Philip, 102–3, 105
Ryerson Press, 98, 110
Ryga, George, 40–41

Scott, F.R., 106
Seven Poems for the Vancouver Festival, 118–19
Shakespeare, William, 40, 97, 101
Shapiro, Karl, 99
Shappiro, Herbert, 94
Shelley, Percy Bysshe, 18, 52, 71, 79, 97, 100, 113, 123–24, 126, 131, 139, 156
Shepard, Sam, 40
Shepp, Archie, 47, 158
Sherrin, Robert, 132
Short Sad Book, A, 48
"Sign, The," 77
Silliman, Ron, 80
Simone, Nina, 158
Sinclair, John, 47
Sir George Williams University, 96–97, 101, 104, 157
Skeat, Walter William, 82
Smith, A.J.M., 106
Smith, Ron, 44
Snodgrass, W.D., 75.
"Songs of Maximus," 67
Sorrentino, Gilbert, 99
Special View of History, The, 126
Spender, Stephen, 75

Spicer, Jack, 90, 109, 118–19
splinterview, 137
Staines, David, 21–22
Stanley, George, 133–36
Stein, Gertrude, 32, 90, 94, 111, 144
Stendhal, 153
Stevenson, Robert Louis, 93
Steveston, 127
Studhorse Man, The, 15
Stylistics, The, 158
Sullen Art, The, 99
Sullivan, Rosemary, 95
Supremes, The, 9
Survival, 101
Swamp Angel, 21

Tads, 133
Tallman, Ellen, 75
Tallman, Karen, 50
Tallman, Warren, 41, 50, 75
Talonbooks, 40, 98
Tanabe, Takao, 109
Taylor, Koko, 158
Tennyson, Alfred, 84–85
Thesen, Sharon, 3
Thomas, Audrey, 82
Thomas, Dylan, 66
Tish, 37, 66, 75–76, 106, 127
Todd, Douglas, 62
translation, 4–5, 7–8
Trial of a City, 128
Trilogy, 67, 96
Trocchi, Alexander, 110
True Mummy, 42
20/20 Gallery, 48
20c Magazine, 48

Ubyssey, The, 37, 74
Ulysses, 32, 84
Under the Volcano, 119–20
University of British Columbia, 37, 73, 74–76, 138, 139

University of Calgary, 47, 96
University of Western Ontario, 47, 96–97
Unquiet Bed, The, 103–4

Vancouver: arts scene, 40–42; in 1950s, 114; in 1960s, 40, 41; in poetry, 114, 115–22, 126–36; poets, 40, 66–67, 74–76, 125, 150–51 (*see also specific poets*); theatre, 40–41, 74; 2010 Olympics, 6
Vancouver: A Poem, 134–36
Vancouver Poems, 127, 129
Véhicule Press, 107
Verlaine, Paul, 134
Victory, 26
visual art, 9, 29, 45, 47, 115–16, 143–44, 159. *See also specific artists*
Vonnegut, Kurt, 153

Wah, Fred, 5, 40, 75, 150
Walmsley, Tom, 40
war movies, 11–12
Washington, Dinah, 158
Waterhouse-Hayward, Alex, 30
Watson, Sheila, 21, 146
Webb, Phyllis, 52, 110
Webb Sisters, 63
Weir, Ian, 41
westerns, 2, 94, 112, 140
Westlake, Donald E., 95
Whalen, Philip, 17
Where Water Comes Together with Other Water, 31
Williams, William Carlos, 17, 66, 71, 80, 124–25, 135, 138

Wilson, Ethel, 21–22
"Windhover, The," 67, 68–72
Wolfe, Thomas, 121
Woodcock, George, 19, 74
Woodman, Ross, 97
Woolf, Douglas, 105
Woolworth's Rattle, The, 47–48
Wordsworth, William, 146, 150
writing: allusion, 87, 88, 129, 131, 135; derivative, 101, 139, 146; and imagination, 113, 115–17; influences, 32, 142–44, 146; intertextuality, 24, 25–26, 84–86, 88, 131, 147; learn by reading, 145; learn by listening, 16; "objectification," 82–84, 86–88; and place, 47, 113, 122–27, 133 (*see also* Vancouver: in poetry); process, 35–36, 37–39, 49, 140–42; and representation, 29–30, 45, 119–20, 122–23, 154–55; revision, 129, 141–42, 151; same as reading, 13, 103, 141–42, 143, 145–47; short stories and novels, 1, 155; takes effort, 84, 144–45; - what you know, 122–24; writer's control of, 122–24, 152–53. *See also* language; poetry; reading; *specific writers*
writing workshops, 139

Xenophon, 95

Yeats, W.B., 115, 139
Yesterday, at the Hotel Clarendon, 85

Zukofsky, Louis, 33